GROWING OLD
IN THE
BRONX

GROWING OLD IN THE BRONX

A MEMOIR BY
Lucille Gold

All names of patients, clients and colleagues have been changed to protect confidentiality.

Printed in the United States of America.

ISBN: 1-59571-109-0
Library of Congress Control Number: 2005939248

Word Association Publishers
205 5th Avenue
Tarentum, PA 15084
www.wordassociation.com

Lucille at age 17 (1937)

Acknowledgements

This memoir would never have been produced without the expertise of Said Ghostine, my computer consultant. His dedication to seeing it written and completed made everything possible. Said believes that computer literacy is especially important for seniors and shares his knowledge with all of us who are open to his generosity.

And my deepest felt thanks to my daughters Jane and Tami, who edited this book. I thank them for more than editing but for their profound interest in the experiences and contributions that women from my generation have had on the 20th century.

My granddaughter Amilca persevered, transcribing my letters from the 1960's for this book; my heartfelt appreciation. And to my granddaughter Robin, who reviewed the entire manuscript, encouraging me to search deeper into my memory to expand on the details and stories of my life, I am moved and grateful.

I have studied many times
The marble which was chiseled for me
A boat with a furled sail at rest in a harbor
In truth it pictures not my destination
But my life.
For love was offered me, and I shrank
From its disillusionment;
Sorrow knocked at my door, but I was afraid;
Ambition called to me, but I dreaded the chances.
Yet all the while I hungered for meaning in my life
And now I know that we must lift the sail
And catch the winds of destiny
Wherever they drive the boat,
To put meaning in one's life may end in madness,
But life without meaning is the torture
Of restlessness and vague desire –
It is a boat longing for the sea and yet afraid.
                              Edgar Lee Masters

Introduction

I have been retired for over fifteen years and now remember back to the very moment when I smiled, drew a deep breath and declared, "Lucille, you can relax now and let go." I had just seen my last patient. I remember the very day. It was December 22, 1989. The time — 9 PM.

I sank down deep into my recliner and thought of Bill, who had just left my office, to go to a party celebrating the Republican's victory in the elections. He was beginning his new life as one of the directors for the Suffolk County Executive Board. I sighed and thought of my new life. After twenty-five years of unrelenting pressure and hard work, I could now finally relax. I had completed my education, struggled to support my children and myself and engaged in the field I loved, serving people as a social worker. I was free at last to pursue my many interests.

I sold my beautiful Long Island home and my motorboat. I gave my wonderful collection of Early American furniture and collectibles to my daughter

Laurie where they are currently displayed in her 150 year-old Colonial farmhouse in the Catskills in upstate New York. All my other remaining possessions, memorabilia, and artwork are in the homes of my daughters, Tami and Jane.

Now unburdened, I moved to Florida and hungrily started exploring all the possibilities my new environment had to offer. There was birding, canoeing, snorkeling and, of course, I would finally be able to paint again, something I had been obliged to give up over the years because of other life commitments and demands.

Birding became the center of my interest. The large watering birds were a special treat. Canoeing along the banks of the soft flowing waters, I came close to the great Blue Heron majestically standing on the shore. Then a flock of egrets would appear, flying off together with a great flurry. At times an Osprey would suddenly startle me, diving from up high, deep into the water to catch its prey. The thrill of this experience, now only a memory, still excites me. I impressed my granddaughter Amilca one day when I named a bird correctly. I said assertively, "It is a Green Heron." In disbelief she referred to my Audubon bird book and in surprise said to her mother Tami, "Ma, Grandma is right. It is a Green Heron!"

I also tackled art. My work in the studio was limited to one day a week where I struggled to produce works of modest worth. Painting just did not come to me as easily as it had in my younger years. My family has my paintings, reflecting 60 years of my artwork from oils to watercolors to pastels, hanging proudly in their homes.

I was a drop out in the tenth grade and only took my GED test at the age of forty. To my amazement, I passed the test on the first try. Shortly after I received my GED I met an old friend from my youth, Johnny Gates, a renowned progressive political leader, at a New Years Eve party. It was 1959. Johnny Gates had been one of the editors of The Daily Worker, a communist newspaper. He was also a General in the Lincoln Brigade, a division of volunteers from around the world who went to fight against fascism in Spain in the mid 1930's. Seeing Johnny brought back wonderful memories of the time when I truly believed we had the power and vision to fight and win against the growing threat of fascism.

During our conversation over champagne he told me of his new adventure with the Ford Foundation's educational program, and that he was about to receive his undergraduate college diploma. He quickly added that he thought it would be a wonderful opportunity for me. "Johnny, me?" Before I could protest he reassured me that I had what it takes — perseverance and resilience. I called for an application the very next day and applied to the Ford Foundation's educational program, although I did not think I had a shot.

A couple of years before I was reacquainted with Johnny Gates, I had decided to volunteer as a recreational therapist at Hillside Hospital, a highly regarded institution for emotionally disturbed people. This was my way of exploring whether the field of social work was for me. As a recreational therapist I was invited to participate in the team approach to treatment. The regular meetings would include the group therapist, the psychiatrist, the individual clinical social worker, the art and dance therapist, the nurse or medical doctor and the recreational therapist. During the case evaluation meetings, I learned diagnostic assessment. At this time an interdisciplinary approach to the entire treatment process was innovative and was an unusual protocol. I flourished in this environment.

Months after applying to the Ford Foundation on a hot summer day, sitting at the kitchen table with my three daughters, I received a phone call that would change my life. I had been selected by the Ford

Foundation to attend their special college program for adults who had achieved professional positions without the benefit of a formal education. After all these years, I still wonder at the fact that I had been selected, one of thirteen who was chosen from over a thousand applications submitted. Imagine my surprise when I went for my formal interview and the professor shook my hand, welcomed me into the program, and said it was a privilege to have me on board.

My difficulty with reading, writing and spelling was acknowledged by my professors and they understood that I had some kind of learning difficulty. This was before learning disabilities were identified as an inherited cognitive syndrome and long before methods of treatment were created. As a child today I would be diagnosed with dyslexia. My professors overlooked this and encouraged me to go on to graduate school in social work. It took ten years of perseverance to get my undergraduate degree and then my Masters of Social Work. On the surface I was pleased with this great accomplishment but deep inside a great deal of self-doubt persisted. Although the years ahead were filled with new concepts in psychology, lying in the recesses of my mind was the disturbing issue of my difficulty with reading and writing. I received help with my written reports, but underneath I was always struggling with the roughed-up edges of my bruised ego. It has always been there to haunt me. Me? Write the story of my life? Impossible! Yet, with all my self-doubt here I am daring to write my memoir.

1

My 'Dark Ages'

The idea of writing my memoir came upon me recently as I was strolling down Kingsbridge Road in the Bronx. Enjoying the sounds and smells of the city, I suddenly realized the irony of the situation. Here I was at eighty-three, growing old in the Bronx, the very place I had fled at twenty-two years old, vowing never to return. I smiled and promised to write of this long voyage one day, so here goes.

A very long time ago, when I was a girl of about fifteen, I made a promise to myself that I would leave the Bronx as soon as I was able to. I hungered for open spaces, trees, lakes, wild vegetation — things that were impossible for me to find in this concrete jungle. I did get out, but in spite of the promise I made to myself, here I am back in the jungle. It was an uphill struggle to leave, not only the city where I felt boxed in by the large brick buildings and lack of sunlight, but also the sadness that surrounded me.

The Great Depression of the 1930's had cast a dark shadow over everything — a shadow that entered my own home and family. My mother died when I was eight years old and was not there to soften the difficulties I faced. The circumstances of her disappearance from my life were not explained to me until many years later, but even as a young child I knew that there was something hidden and shameful about it. Something I was not allowed to question or talk about.

To make matters worse, my father was a very depressed widower with little energy for his four children — Arthur, Vivian, Raymond and me. He awoke early every day to leave for work and didn't return until late in the evening. My father didn't encourage me to take advantage of the many opportunities available in my community that might have brightened my dismal existence. Years later I could see how other children growing up in the Bronx even thrived during the Depression. At that time the community centers, such as The Bronx House in Pelham Bay, were gathering the youth together for social groups, sporting activities and other clubs, where special interests and hobbies were developed. In addition, there was the 4 H Club, the Girls and the Boys Clubs.

But for me, there was nothing — no warmth extended to me by neighbors or teachers. The memory of my street with no open space to play in remains vivid. No one in my family ever asked to see my report cards and there was no supervision or interest given to anything I did.

When my older brother Arthur was fifteen, he went to live with my mother's three sisters, Aunts Gussie, Frieda and Regina, in Manhattan. As a result of this move, Arthur became very distant from the rest of the family, a distance that has lasted our lifetime. The rest of us, (Vivian, who was thirteen years old, me, at eight years old and Raymond, an infant), had to be cared for by housekeepers. We had one housekeeper after another. I don't remember any of their names or anything about them. The only memory I have is that there was no warmth.

Faced with this difficulty, my father chose to have all of us live with his sister Dora's family in one big apartment on Southern Blvd. in the East Bronx. It was a big, bright, elevated building and a relief to share a warm home with my cousins. This is one of the fondest memories I have of family life. Although I loved everything about living with my aunt Dora and her family, my sister Vivian resented the situation, wanting to be the head of our household.

I hated the constant fighting between Vivian and Aunt Dora. There was so much tension that after three years my father gave in to Vivian's demands to leave. We moved again, this time to a dark and cramped apartment in the West Bronx. The plan was that Vivian would take over the responsibility of the family. Finally Vivian could be the boss. But, just as soon as we moved, she met Myron who became her boyfriend and her whole life. At eighteen, she married him and moved out. It became my task to take over the responsibility for the family. I was fourteen.

I owned one blouse, one skirt and one pair of shoes. Each night I would wash my shirt, trying to keep it as white as possible, and then place it on the radiator to dry. I cannot recall who fed us during this time. The only exposure I had to what was happening in the outside world came from the little radio in our bedroom and what I heard and saw on the streets. There were men standing on corners selling apples for a nickel or sweet potatoes for a dime. Raymond and I had other plans for any coins we could find. When we came upon a nickel we would always buy a Drake's sponge cake with white icing on top, sprinkled with shredded coconut. With delight at our good fortune we prepared ourselves for this infrequent but always anticipated treat. No words were necessary as we found our ruler and one of us would measure and cut the cake in half while the other looked on to prevent cheating. That two and a half inch piece of cake is still burned in my memory.

I did not speak out then, but I remember a vow I took one day, at the age of sixteen. Though I have very few memories of those years, I can see myself clearly looking out the window and making a promise to dedicate my life to helping children and others who were overlooked and neglected.

During my early adolescence my life brightened when I became close friends with a girl who lived on the next block. Shirley and I became buddies, and after school, hating to part, we would walk each other home, going back and forth from her house to mine. Slowly we extended our time together with my visits to her ground floor apartment. She lived there with her mother and six older sisters. This loving group of mother and children caring for one another reminded me of my time with my aunt Dora. And to my surprise and joy, they took me in as one of their own, sharing the little they had.

The kitchen at the Fogelsons' home was the center of all activity and, no matter what time of day, you could find someone around to talk to and share a meal. There was always food to eat because Mrs. Fogelson cooked large pots of stew every Friday for anyone who cared to partake. The pot was heated over and over again and the flavor was forever improving.

The children were made fatherless soon after Shirley's birth. Mrs. Fogelson, as I always called her, supported her family by selling hats and notions in the front room of their storefront apartment. Notions were all of the items, like thread, needles and ribbons, needed for making garments. Selling notions was a common industry, as homemakers often sewed their families clothing. The older Fogelson children worked after school to help out with the finances.

Mrs. Fogelson was always getting involved in one venture or another. As an independent woman, she ran a singles club for middle-aged adults like herself. She certainly was a powerful role model for her children, and they profited. All seven girls were well educated, three had even gone to college, and that was an accomplishment in those days for anyone, particularly women.

I was particularly drawn to Shirley's sister Dorothy, who was considered "counter-culture." Though she never spoke of her beliefs, I think she was a socialist. She wore her dark brown hair in braids and looked like a beautiful native Indian woman. Married to Sol and still living at home, she was proud of her body and taught us to welcome our physical maturity from childhood to womanhood. Dorothy would speak to Shirley and me about sex and explained that it was a beautiful experience between two people. She and Sol would lie on their bed, openly affectionate. I was awed, as a naive adolescent, to see the chemistry they shared, as well as the sheer delight they felt from just being in each other's company. Up to that point, I had never seen or experienced affection like that. Remember, this was in the mid 1930's when to even talk about sex was taboo.

Dorothy took me to my first May Day parade when I was seventeen. I knew nothing about the significance of this event. But before my eyes, right in the middle of Union Square, I saw thousands of men, women and children joyously chanting and singing. I learned that May Day was a celebration of the accomplishments of the working class and that this celebration took place all over the world. And of all things, Dorothy brought carrot and celery sticks for us to munch on. Those were the meat and potato days. Nutrition? What was that? Diet to lose weight? What was that? We hardly had enough to eat. Of course, now it's not unusual to see me snacking on carrots and celery when I am on a diet yet again.

And then there was Dorothy's friend Ernest, who must have seen something unusual in me. He bought me a beginner's set of art supplies and, so equipped, I attended an art class for the first time, where I began painting with oils. Ernest introduced me to the theater, museums, and other exciting cultural, scientific and political happenings in Manhattan. I was dazzled by everything I encountered, and the world kept opening up. Why Ernest chose me for this privilege I never questioned. Years later he told me that he thought I had an inquisitive mind worthy of his attention. On refection, I think I was his Pygmalion. Bernard Shaw's heroine was a wild one from the East End of London who he fashioned into a lady. Lucky for me, I never became a lady.

Another deep memory is when I first saw the Hoovervilles along the Hudson River. The homeless built little hovels made up of old pieces of metal and cardboard, one leaning on the next, along the bank of the river. What held them up is still a mystery to me. By 1931, tens of thousands of New Yorkers had been evicted from their homes, and often their friends and families were also suffering and unable to help them. These Hoovervilles popped up all over the country, but the largest was in New York City. It is no wonder that here is where radical political thinking was fomented. Hooverville was named after President Hoover who, during the Great Depression of the 1930's, looked the other way and let the entire nation suffer. We needed help and the federal government failed us. Organizing and fighting for a more equitable distribution of wealth gave us a sense of hope and empowerment. Socialism was the answer by its very definition.

All around me I witnessed heartache. It took different forms and many innovative ways to handle it. There was my friend Esther's barrel. Everyone in her family had his or her own barrel, where they kept their meager belongings. Each time the family was evicted from an apartment they just moved their barrels to the next apartment. The terrible sadness I saw in my father's face and in the faces of my friends' fathers still haunt me to this day.

My father, Max, was a sub-contractor in the garment industry. The manufacturer would get most of the profits and the contractor would get the small amount that remained. I remember my father bringing home bundles of cloth for our relatives who lived near us. They would sit, bent over their sewing machines, and work at attaching one piece of cloth to another, creating garments. Tanta Honnie, my aunt, and her husband would raise their heads, smile at me, and then quickly return to their task. My cut of the spoils was the one-dollar bill I would get from my father before he went off to work, that is if I got up in time to catch him. The dollar was our lifeline for survival. I would buy one half pound of beef and hope that the butcher would throw in some bones for soup. Then I was off to buy potatoes and soup greens for three pennies. If I felt rich, I would buy the five-cent bunch of greens. Now to the grocery store for mixed dry beans and yet another store for rye bread. Then it was back to the apartment where all these precious ingredients were dumped into a pot of water. In a few hours the boiling concoction would be ready. My father got a bowl of soup and on another plate the meat, potatoes and beans. Raymond and I would share the rest. That is, unless my sister Vivian and her husband Myron appeared, which they often did, and then the remaining soup would be shared among the four of us. Many years later I learned that there were days, sometimes weeks, when Vivian and Myron lived on peanuts and tea alone.

In 1936 I learned about the Civil War in Spain and that many young men from the United States were secretly going to Spain to fight against Fascism. I went to many parties for young boys who were volunteering to go to Spain to fight with the Lincoln Brigade. At the same time there was a demonstration in Washington, DC where unemployed Americans converged on the capital to demand relief. Young people around me were buzzing about Stalin and Trotsky. Folk singers, like Woody Guthrie, were everywhere and new ideas were communicated through their lyrics. There was talk about the need for radical change in our government. This seemed to offer me some hope. One day, with this new positive and hopeful stimulation, I passed the storefront of the Young Communist League (YCL) and dared to take a big step. I walked in and, right then and there, I joined. It was a lark, and I did it on my own without discussing it with anyone. Much that was discussed there was new to me and over my head, but it was a good way to meet people, especially young men. Among them was Morty. He was the vice-president of his local trade union and quite prominent in the YCL. This impressive information was not lost on me, and I began spending more and more time with Morty.

Although I was attracted to Morty, my boyfriend of many years was Sam. Sam was fun, loved to banter and, along with our friends, we had wonderful times together. He was still in high school, though and had no money, hardly someone who could give me the security I needed.

While all this was evolving, I felt pressure from my mother's elitist sisters. Gussie, Frieda and Regina lived in Manhattan on 87th Street and Columbus Avenue in a brownstone, which was considered then, as it is today, a mark of economic success. My mother's three sisters, who never married, were the only consistent mother role models in my life from my early childhood through my middle adult years.

I often visited my aunts in this brownstone as a child. I can still smell the starch from their white linen sheets. They were so white, the likes of which I had never seen before. To this day I have seen many a white sheet, but never as bright and as crisp as theirs. Before I was allowed to climb onto the fluffed up enormous bed, I was given a bath and my head examined for lice. I still cringe at the memory of the humiliation I felt. But after the examination, which I usually passed, I found pleasure in the Ponds cold cream I discovered in their bathroom. I would apply a small amount of the soft white cream onto my hands and rub it over my entire body. Somewhere in the deep recesses of my mind I must have taken note of this wonderful experience and as a result, you will always find Ponds cold cream on my makeup shelf next to Estee Lauder's wrinkle reducing foundation formula and Elizabeth Arden's marvelous organic herb lotion.

My aunts' influence on me was substantial and I felt the pressure of their standards. I had a great deal of climbing to do. Though I was in love with Sam, he was still just a high school student. On the other hand, Morty, who only went as far as the ninth grade, was a skilled dye maker with a job that paid $35 weekly, which was a most respectable income in those days. My aunts saw in him a good potential husband for me. Although pulled in so many directions, I chose to marry Morty. He represented financial stability, he was a respected community leader, and he would be a partner to share my newly found political interests. Like so many of my generation, I looked to marriage for independence and to escape from my father's depressing home.

And so a life long conflict began. On one hand I had made a commitment to work for those like myself who were wounded and neglected by society. And then there was the pull of my Hungarian born aunts, Gussie, Regina, and Frieda, who had developed successful businesses as dressmakers in the United States. They urged me to climb the ladder of success and achieve their version of the American Dream — power, prestige and privilege.

Before Morty and I were married, I worked as a seamstress in a small shop and felt isolated by the nature of the work and the environment. So I told this to Morty and he helped me get a job working on an assembly line at the folding box factory where he worked. Immediately, he encouraged me to join the union where I became active. I loved it. There were people and laughter and the work was actually fun. This was a moment of great happiness for me— when I believed Morty and I were building a life together.

I turned 21 years old in February of 1941 and talk of war was in the air. Morty was 25, and along with all of our male friends, was drafted. It was just a few months after we married, and off he went to military training for the Armed Forces. We had no time to even get to know one another, let alone build a marital relationship. Now alone, living with other girls whose husbands had also left for the war, I was encouraged by the YCL to do my part in the effort to defeat fascism by working in a factory making weapons for our men fighting the war in Europe.

I understood, only in an abstract way, that Hitler and the Nazi Party were executing the Jewish population throughout Europe. For some reason I could not absorb this reality. On June 22, 1941, Hitler unleashed the full power of his military machine against the two thousand mile Russian frontier and fiercely attacked the Soviet Union. The Soviet Union was a place and an ideal that I believed in. It was then that I realized our hope of spreading this peaceful socialist vision throughout the world was in jeopardy. With the Nazis in power, this would no longer be possible.

My girlfriends and I were encouraged to participate and then organized to travel to areas where manufacturing jobs were in desperate need. This included preparing the metal for guns. Elmira, New York was chosen for me by the YCL, and Lottie was selected as my partner. Within days we were on our way to organize for the war effort and I was excited and nervous all at the same time.

In 1941, Elmira was a sleepy upstate town and not yet recovered from the Depression. If there was a special role that the YCL had wanted us to fill besides working for the war effort they never told us and we never asked. Thinking back to those days as a young Communist, I question why the FBI created such hysteria and incited the witch-hunt. We were young, uneducated and naive — hardly political conspirators.

Out of the Bronx at last and into the countryside we went. The green grass, the rolling hills, the fruit trees were all new to me and just as I imagined them to be. I was happy in this new paradise. For the first time in my life I could skip and run with the breeze blowing through my long hair. I felt light and alive. And I was feeling productive as I worked, just "one of the boys", grinding down metal to be made into guns which would be used to kill young men. I was now earning $60 a week. As a factory worker in the folding box industry in the Bronx I had earned $16 a week. I learned soon enough the reason for the disparity in pay between a paper factory and a gun factory.

War was a wonderful opportunity for the upper class to capture a new industry — the war industry. And war is always beneficial to a capitalist economy. I went to Elmira to work in the war industry as my way to fight against fascism and to defend the Soviet Union. At the same time, special interest groups, the corporate executives, put pressure on Congress to grant lucrative contracts to big corporations like Bendics, the company I worked for in Elmira. Not satisfied with this windfall, these companies had written into the contracts a *Cost Plus Agreement*. This agreement meant that a corporation would receive from the United States government 10% more than the actual cost to produce the product. If it took a longer time to make a gun or a fighter airplane the corporation benefited.

I learned much about this the day I was called on the carpet for my production record. Proud to help the war effort, I was working very fast and over producing. The complaint from my supervisor was that I was not polishing each piece more carefully. I protested, but to no avail. They came back with a fast response. I was charged with working too fast to do the job right. The company wanted me to produce less in order to have their profitable contracts continued. I finally understood and promised to do my work with "greater care." I did not need Karl Marx to explain capitalism to me, I was learning on the assembly line.

Elmira's working class got a shot in the arm, and I too was a benefactor. I remember my first paycheck. Actually, I don't recall the check at all for it was cashed the very next day. But I remember what I purchased with the money. I bought a make-up travel case. It was a plastic brown satchel that opened to reveal compartments with bottles of all sizes, I presume to hold creams and powders. I don't remember filling them since I didn't wear anything on my face, but I was very proud of it and showed it off to the family back in the Bronx. To this day, I don't quite understand why I made that purchase. On reflection, I think it might have represented my embracing the new life ahead of me — a life of expansion, adventure, new places, and new people. Little did I know at the time, my life would turn into a long stretch of wandering, searching for a place to settle and dig deep roots. But the sense of adventure I began to feel back in Elmira endured, and I still get excited when I encounter new situations that require changes of scenery, people and cultures.

I certainly know why my second purchase was made. In my childhood, I remember seeing Jean Harlow on the screen eating chocolate candies. Some were filled with cream, some with marshmallows and then there were the ones filled with delicious caramel. Harlow would casually discard a piece if she didn't like the filling. So was born another dream. And I would some day be able to fulfill this dream. Now the time had come. With my newfound riches I bought that box of chocolates. I didn't share a single piece with my roommate Lottie. However, I did deviate from Harlow's behavior and could never discard a piece of these delectable sweet bonbons. Instead, I would hide it at the bottom of the box to be eaten some day in the future when I had depleted every last flavored piece of chocolate. As the years went by I continued to buy that same box of chocolates.

The people I was meeting in Elmira were different from the people I had known in the Bronx. Before going there, I do not think I knew anyone who wasn't Jewish. And here I was at a party with Norwegians who invited Lottie and me for a hot bath at their home. Shocked, I ran to Bernie and Kate, the YCL organizers who we lived with, who explained what a hot bath was, Norwegian style — a tiny wooden house that is well heated by a wood burning fire under large rocks. When water is thrown on the rocks steam fills the tiny house. Reluctantly we accepted the invitation, and, getting into the spirit of it all, we were pounded with a long switch. We learned this was to stimulate the body and to get rid of the toxins harbored within. It was all very scary but Lottie and I endured for we were, after all, connecting to the people we worked with in the factory.

Another experience I treasure was learning how to shoot, yes, shoot a gun. I'm not sure if it was a rifle or a pistol. But I do know it was thrilling. A friend from the factory invited us to his backyard and taught Lottie and me how to use a gun, and we were off — shooting away. In time, I became an excellent marksman and from then on it was my sport of choice.

Finally out of the Bronx, the only environment I had known, these new experiences — bowling, horseback riding, hiking and connecting to nature enthralled me. This connection to nature opened me to a deep internal joy that has always remained within me.

But there were moments when I would miss the Bronx — the fresh rye bread and prune Danish. From time to time Bernie would bring back these delicacies when he went down to the big city. Lox and herring added to the festive spirit of those special occasions.

The night shift at the factory was a bit hard to get used to, but eventually I did. While we walked home after a night of tiring and demanding work, Lottie and I would pick berries in the open fields. We walked as the sun rose surrounded by the scent of morning dew. I had never seen berries actually growing on a bush. As a matter of fact, I had never seen any fruit growing in its own habitat. One morning, unaware that we were walking on someone's property, the homeowner chastised us for picking berries in her yard. When I lived in the city, I imagined that open land belonged to everyone. On some level the world around me was still a mystery. How could land be private? At this point, I could take nothing for granted.

Of course, by now I have accepted the fact that land has great value and is in great demand. In my seventies I joined The Nature Conservancy to protect it. This organization purchases important parcels of land, which would otherwise go to developers or be sold off to individuals. I have even put my marker on a piece of land in Florida called Blowing Rocks. That is the only piece of land I own now and I cannot even walk on it because it goes in and out with the tide.

I had moved to Elmira to do political work, however, the unexpected happened. I had landed in a new environment where I touched nature for the first time and felt a kinship to the world. My new pastimes were disheartening for my aunts, who thought tennis should be my chosen sport. It was hard to explain to them that, in fact, I was living the life of a rural factory worker and they should be patient with me and eventually I would climb up their ladder.

I was always "brought up short" by one aunt or another and in no time Aunt Regina told me Elmira was known for its notorious prison, the worst in the state and not a good place to come from. Aunt Regina just had to mention this on one of my visits home. My aunt's pressure and influence on me led me to always look for "a place that was good to come from." So Elmira wasn't a "great place to come from." I tried to ignore my aunts' comments, but their constant judgment was always burning inside me.

Back at my job in Elmira, my boss accused me of having a sexual relationship with a black man. I did admit he was a good friend, but so was his wife. The very concept of an "affair" was completely foreign to me. This rumor was spread throughout the plant by management, so that in a short time they could fire me without having to be concerned with my co-workers supporting me. It was the 1940's and most white working-class Americans were deeply prejudiced and the idea of an interracial sexual relationship and an affair, to top it off, was taboo. So this was their way of getting rid of me in silence. In reality, I was singled out because I, one of a very small group, had joined the organizing team that was trying to form a union in the factory. I was fired. But no remorse, after all, Elmira was "a place that was not good to come from." So said my aunts.

The Young Communist League then directed me to a Safe House in Syracuse, New York. All they gave me were the names of people in charge of the Safe House and a phone number. There were no other instructions or guidance. I applied on my own to work as a metal grinder at a manufacturing company. I walked into the noisy front office wearing the fashionable fur coat that my father had given me. Max had purchased Vivian and me inexpensive fur coats that had become popular in New York City. So here I was in Syracuse, a small city still suffering the affects of the Depression. I was 21 years old, unaware of how attractive I was, and so naive. All over the country, women were needed to replace the men who had gone off to the war. Though I must have stood out like a sore thumb, I was hired and immediately put in the tool room where I became a toolmaker, a coveted job at the factory. After just a few months, I finished my apprenticeship and was officially considered a skilled toolmaker. Prior to the war, a worker would have to first be carefully selected for this position, and then trained for four years.

What stands out in my store of memories is the shame I felt as I worked along side Harry, a caring older white man. He was about sixty-five years old, but looked much older. Because of the war he had been asked to come out of retirement and go back to the factory where he had been a metal grinder for years. Harry had never been offered the opportunity to become a skilled toolmaker. And here he was, continuing his menial tasks alongside me, who because of the war effort and the lack of skilled male workers, had been fast-tracked up the ranks.

I was doing my part in the struggle to defeat Hitler. I was a new bride without a husband. I was moving from community to community. All the war action was taking place thousands of miles away. And at that time, none of my friends or family members had been wounded or killed. Now as I think back to that period of time, I realize I was very emotionally detached. Sure, my world had been changed. My life as a new wife was put on hold and because my husband was stationed in Mississippi and not in the line of fire, I was not worried about his safety. I also blocked out the horror of what was happening to the Jewish people throughout Europe.

I blocked and detached. I had learned these survival tools at a very early age. I know it started with the hidden shame surrounding my mother's death. For years I wondered what had happened to her, but I was too frightened to ask. And no one in my family would speak about my mother, or for that matter, speak about anything of an intimate nature. It was as though she never existed.

While in Syracuse I discovered the university up on the hill and became aware that there were people my age in college studying. I envied them. As a high school drop out, I knew I could not walk up there but I secretly wanted to be there — in the sororities, having all the experiences and fun they seemed to be having.

This was at a time when the division between the lower and upper classes was even greater than it is today. Here is where I learned more about class. As a worker, I was not eligible to join the uppers. My father had very little money, spoke with an accent and my family was from the Jewish ghetto in the Bronx. I now had something new to aspire to. Somehow I had to become educated, upper class, as well as come from "a place that was good to come from."

Suddenly I was called back to the Bronx. My sister needed my help so that she could stay in bed during her third attempt at a pregnancy. I moved in with Vivian, Myron and my brother Raymond, now 13 years old. Within the first few weeks of my return, I had to go to Raymond's middle school when a teacher demanded to see his mother. I remember Raymond telling me hilariously how he yelled back at his teacher, "I have no mother, so there!"

I went to the school and was told that Raymond was failing every subject. In a cold and mean spirited way the teacher went on to say that the school did not think he would graduate. She recommended he be sent to a military academy. I slowly walked home with Raymond, completely stunned by the teacher's words. I began to feel anger welling up in my body. "Raymond you're not stupid, you can do anything with your hands," I said. "Change a lock, realign doors, and fix furniture. You are so mechanical! You are so smart! Maybe the 3R's are not for us, but we can surely accomplish a lot with our hands."

Myron immediately found Raymond a job as a plumber's assistant where he flourished. From that day on, Raymond never returned to school where there was no guidance or understanding of his learning disabilities. His innate intelligence and mechanical talents blossomed as a plumber. He found the field that he and his future family would make into a thriving Bronx business with commercial commissions in all five boroughs.

On December 9th, 1941 Vivian gave birth to Freddy, two days after the Japanese attacked our ships stationed in Pearl Harbor. President Roosevelt had declared war on December 8th. An event as wonderful as the birth of my first-born nephew was diminished by the shock of this sudden attack.

A few months following Freddy's birth I got a job at a factory in Manhattan. Again, I worked in the war industry as a toolmaker for two years. During this time Morty was never sent overseas to fight in the war but had to continue living in an army barrack in Mississippi. We thought the war was winding down and we decided I should join him in Mississippi.

What an awakening! Jim Crow, the systematic practice of discriminating against and suppressing black people, was in full force. It was more than the separate restrooms and water fountains that upset me. It was the beaten down demeanor of the black people. While walking on the street a black man was required by this social code to get off the sidewalk to let a white person pass. It was against military law for a white soldier to be friends with a black person. Morty had to skirt the town to meet, undercover, with his black friends. The blatant trashing of black people was unbearable, a nightmare.

Morty was stationed in Jackson, Mississippi where I soon found a government job at a local factory as a flat metal grinder. The war continued but Morty was never deployed and we lived together for about two years. Eventually I became pregnant and Morty and I decided that it would be best for me to return to the Bronx where I would have the support of my family. I thought that Morty was not going to be sent to fight in Europe and he would be home with me very soon.

Raymond and I set up a new apartment across the street from where Vivian and Myron lived. By this time I was four months pregnant and loved and welcomed all the changes in my body. It was 1945, the war ended and the boys began coming home, but not Morty. He had been in Mississippi for the entire duration of the war and now he was being sent to Germany as an MP (Military Police). We were just never given a chance.

Surprisingly, at the same time Raymond decided to enlist in the army. He was only seventeen and needed permission from Vivian and me. There was no way that I would let the military take someone else from my life. We denied him permission and to placate him we bought him an old beat up Ford, and so a new adventure began. It was one of the only cars on the block, and many a Sunday, we would all pile in — Vivian, Myron and their children. By now there were two boys, Freddy and Teddy. The car was so small that we had to tie the lunch to the outside fender and off we would go, with Raymond majestically driving us to the countryside.

On September 17, 1945, I gave birth to my first daughter, Jane, with my father by my side. Through the 18 hours of labor my father made all the difference in keeping me grounded. During those years, it was not unusual for women to give birth with their husbands overseas.

When I woke from the effects of the anesthesia I was in a state of euphoria and kept calling out, "I have a baby, I have a baby girl." I was overjoyed with the prospect of having my very own family. Within hours after the birth of Jane, I hemorrhaged and then had to remain in the hospital for ten days. In a weakened state, I went home with my baby in my arms, to my fourth-floor walk up. Frightened by the responsibility of this new little life and having no skills and no models to guide me, I fumbled along relying heavily on my sister to help me through the first difficult months. For years Vivian had been cast in the role of the mother I never had. But now, she became my teacher, my confidant and my best friend. And Raymond became the head-of-the-household.

Shortly after Jane's birth, Morty sent me a Leika still camera from Germany. Not uncommon in war situations, Morty and all his MP buddies entered the private homes of German citizens and confiscated anything they considered valuable. So I inherited the camera of a German. At that time this was acceptable to me. With anticipation and delight, my whole family would open up all the packages Morty sent us. I am now ashamed that during a war I could sink so low as to find this acceptable.

Up to this time, I had only seen and used a simple box camera. At first Raymond and I took photograph after photograph, learning about all the possibilities this new camera offered — focus, f-stop, depth of field. Of course our subject matter was our new treasure, Jane. Raymond, always technically creative and enterprising, conjured up the idea of using the camera as an enlarger. He developed a dark room in our apartment and there without any light, laughing away at our ignorance, we learned the art of black and white still photography. We experimented with oils on Jane's body to create shadows and then used light to enhance the images.

When Jane was a year old Morty finally came home, but he was strangely different — not the young vital man he had been when he left. During his long absence, my family circle had become Raymond, my brother, who I doted over and adored, my absolutely beautiful 12 month-old daughter, Jane, and Vivian's family across the street. It seems obvious now that when Morty returned he must have felt like an outsider. We were two strangers forced into this strained situation. As time went on, the tension between Morty and I grew, as did his resentment of the love and closeness I felt for my sister and brother.

In addition to all of this, Morty had suffered from a deep depression while he was in Mississippi. He had so desperately wanted to fight against fascism and for the liberation of our people. However, because he was a card carrying Communist, he, like many other Communists, was never deployed during wartime. This insult was heightened by the fact that his older brother was a celebrated veteran of the Abraham Lincoln Brigade that fought in Spain in the 1930's. When Morty returned from Germany he slowly told me about his experiences in the death camps, cleaning up corpuses, attending to the wounded and dying soldiers and the massive destruction all around. These images continued to haunt him long after his return.

In the 1940's we did not understand these things. Many years later this phenomenon was labeled — Post Traumatic Stress Disorder. Not understanding the change in him, I tried to accept his detachment and sullenness, as I also struggled to accept an unfulfilling marriage. By 1948 Morty and I had another daughter, Laurie.

In a foreshadowing of our irresolvable conflict over

how to build our lives together, my husband was completely indifferent to my complaints about walking up and down so many flights of stairs and the difficulty of raising two children in a tiny Bronx apartment. Raymond was still living with us and I cannot even remember where everyone slept.

I was becoming increasingly more isolated by the physical limitations of living on the fourth-floor. During those early years of telephone technology, we were unable to get a telephone because the service was in short supply. Raymond, with his inventiveness, found the solution. He was famous for overcoming most obstacles facing us in that apartment. He threw an electrical line from Vivian's building across Grand Avenue to ours and connected a large battery to each end. My brother Arthur, who was an advanced electrical engineer in Washington, DC, gave Raymond two old telephone receivers that were connected to the electrical wire at each end. Raymond then attached two buttons, one in my apartment and one in Vivian's. This way we could ring each other. It was a limited phone system but it worked for my sister and me.

When I did a food shopping I would leave everything in the baby carriage in the basement. When Raymond returned home from work, he put the bags of food on the dumb waiter (a small and clumsy, manual elevator used to carry garbage from one floor to another) and screamed up to me on the fourth floor. I would hoist the rope attached to the dumb waiter until the packages appeared in our kitchen. And then there was the rope with a small container attached hanging from our window for the small things Raymond would buy me before he went off to work.

When I was pregnant with my third child, Tami, I dragged Morty kicking and screaming away from the Bronx to a garden apartment in Astoria, Queens right next to giant gas tanks. Not much of a view, but at least I no longer had to carry one child as I pushed the other up those endless steps.

My next project was to get us to the countryside. I persevered and, with the help of my father's one thousand dollars and the GI bill's no interest loans for American veterans, we were able to buy a home in Levittown, Long Island. Levittown was a pioneer suburb in Nassau County for working class families like us. We finally had a home of our own and Raymond, now married, and Vivian soon followed us. We lived within blocks of each other and together we were raising our children and improving our homes. We were the classic tight knit family completely involved with each other's lives.

This was the first time since my mother's death, over 20 years ago, that I felt rooted and safe. Although the houses were modest and all looked alike, dotting acres of potato fields, I was in heaven. By then I had given up hope of ever coming from an upscale "place that was good to come from."

We all worked together. I planted vegetables and put beautiful evergreens in the front yard. Morty and I learned how to build a spare room in the attic — first the beams, then the dry walls, then the spackling compound. We needed to dig our own water wells and with Raymond's skill as a plumber, we went from one house to another accomplishing the task. Myron supervised the electrical work required while Vivian and I were ever there acting as gofers.

Raymond's wife, Starr, was a stunning and creative woman who, with her black hair and black eyes, was a perfect compliment to my handsome, blue eyed, fair-haired brother. Artistically oriented, Starr was always creating something unusual, using old items and found objects for practical and decorative purposes. She wanted a large family and added Reed, Hale, Evan, Lida, Quinn, Fern and Hunt to our expanding family. Starr liked the idea of giving her children unusual but simple names, usually having just one syllable.

Weekends would find us, the whole family with the new friends we made, working for the United Nations Association and Peaceful Alternatives. Of course my father and his wife, Sylvia, were included. By this time, 10 years after he married her, my father's wife had finally been promoted and was now called Grandma Sylvia. No matter whose home we gathered at, we always ate spaghetti and salad. We were living on a budget (not enough money for meat) and I still have our tax returns from those years to prove it. Believe it or not, we had a beautiful home (we paid $8,000 for the home, $1,000 as a down payment, and $53 for the monthly mortgage), a car, and the entire Long Island countryside on a salary of six thousand and five hundred dollars a year.

Behind the scenes we were playing cops and robbers with the FBI. McCarthy was whipping up the country with anti-communist propaganda. It was the early 1950's and the Smith Act, outlawing the Communist Party, had become the letter of the law, which made us suspect and open to arrest. I had become more conscious of the growing tension around our political beliefs while living in Astoria. One of my neighbors had seen the "Left" books and journals that we had around our house. From that day on many people in the community distanced themselves from us. Strange as it may sound, this never seemed to upset me. I accepted it and continued with my normal daily chores – children, shopping and housework.

The Red Scare was at its height. Levittown was unique and we were lucky because many of our neighbors were progressive and some had a humanistic worldview. Although it was not a racially mixed town, Levittown was culturally and economically diverse. There was a social worker down the block from us and our next-door neighbor was a police officer. It was common to have a car mechanic living next to a schoolteacher. My neighbors reported to us when they saw strange men taking the license plate numbers of people visiting us. We were very careful that all "Left" publications were sent to us in unmarked envelopes.

I remember one day while I was living in Levittown, I opened the local newspaper and to my shock, I saw my name. The American Legion had singled me out as a danger to the community because I was the leader of Peaceful Alternatives. Oh, I was mad. There was no mention of the fact that I was one of the founding members of the American Association of the United Nations, which I am still proud of. But I was not frightened.

When Jane was eight-years old she began hearing about the "evil Communists" from teachers and students at her school. What was she to believe about her parents? At the same time Morty and I joined an organizing campaign to expose the discriminating housing practices throughout Long Island, which prevented Blacks from moving into our community. One of our tactics was to have a white married couple rent a house and then have a Black family move into it. We were working with Black families who were committed to revealing the growing Red Lining of Long Island. Often when a Black family moved in, neighbors called the police and the family was immediately evicted. All of us who were involved with this campaign understood ahead of time that our objective was to expose this racist housing practice. On one occasion, Jane was with us during an eviction, which involved a Black family with two children. I wasn't aware until years later how frightening and traumatic this experience was for her. Jane lived with fear and secrecy.

Myron lost his job at the Navy Yards in Brooklyn on the grounds that he was disloyal. He fought to get his job back and was relieved to be rehired. Then, after only two days he was fired again for being a security risk. When the Freedom of Information Act passed in 1966, we requested Myron's FBI report. We were dismayed, but not completely surprised, to find his files were filled with accusations about his affiliation with me, which was what had resulted in him being fired from his job at the Navy Yards. One of the charges against him was Raymond's clever and innocent telephone hook-up between our two apartments in the Bronx. They claimed that it was a spy apparatus.

It's strange that during this highly politically active period I wasn't frightened by any of the threats to our freedom, our jobs and our privacy. I went about doing the things I had to do — shopping, cleaning, caring for my children, trying to continue with my artwork and working for what I believed in.

But I didn't entirely bury my head in the sand as I began to recognize the growing danger ahead. In the event of my arrest, I hid my children's birth certificates and vaccination records to protect my children from being taken by the government. I invited my father to my home and showed him where I had hidden everything and simply told him to pick up my children and the documents if he heard of my arrest. He never said a word, he just nodded, and in spite of his strong anti-communist sentiment, he kissed me and we left together for Sunday dinner at Vivian's. We had a few visits from the FBI, but the CIA was busy elsewhere. In those days, they were off toppling democratically elected governments in Latin America and in other parts of the world.

Although there was enormous political tension in the air, I loved living in Levittown with my large extended family. But I did pay a heavy price for my personal happiness. Morty was very conflicted that we had left the Bronx and Queens for the countryside. For him, it was giving up the struggle for socialism. He berated me for my so-called bourgeois ways. Somehow, having children, owning a house and getting pleasure in this environment was a violation that represented my lack of social and political commitment. Nothing I said could appease him. Right then and there we should have faced the fact that we simply had different visions for our future. I believed I could continue my dedication to serving people, and still enjoy living in Levittown among working class people. Having a home and children seemed to me an appropriate goal for everyone, even communists. After all, wasn't that what we were working for? We should have separated but instead he wore me down. I guess at some level I felt guilty.

It was 1953, my life came to a stand still. The horror of this time is indescribable. Julius and Ethel Rosenberg were on trail for treason as Soviet spies. They were found guilty and sentenced to death in the electric chair. We were all numb. Everything in our lives stopped as we waited day after day, fighting for a stay of execution. On the final day, I was in my home with my family standing around the radio hoping, as the minutes drew closer to the time of execution, that they would be granted a stay. Then we heard the announcement, "Ethel is being walked to the electric chair. She is walking in silence and as her last act she kissed the matron." Julius followed shortly after. There was complete silence in my home. I turned off the radio.

The next day my daughters and I went to the funeral with my close friends. At the cemetery, we created a big circle around the newly dug gravesites and stood in defiance, honoring Julius and Ethel's bravery. Morty went to work and completely withdrew from me, from the world.

The execution of the Rosenberg's weighed heavily on me, as did Morty's increased rejection of me. I became more and more depressed. Finally, I gave in. I followed the rules of the patriarchal family and eventually he got his way. I gave up, caved in, and we moved away from Levittown and my family, closer to New York City and Morty's place of work.

2
My 'Enlightenment'

We chose a house in Franklin Square, not for its charm, but it was, at $21,000, within our price range and near shopping and schools. The house had a small backyard, just large enough to fit a picnic table. There was a small garden and a large side yard with a swing set. Morty's practicality reigned and I passively stood by.

The shock of the move was overwhelming and on the very first day, in the house, I felt something break in me as the movers carried the freezer down to the basement. I suffered a mental breakdown.

It was labeled a breakdown but, in fact, it was a break out. All the suppressed terror of my childhood, the rage at my mistreatment in the years following my mother's death and years of being a wanderer came pouring out. I suddenly became unable to tolerate my husband's trashing of my dreams for a home, a family and roots. The eruption reached a boiling point and the feelings lying dormant inside me came to the surface. I cried, raged and withdrew to my bed for days at a time. Also in the mix, there was the shock at the exposure of Stalin's atrocities. My life's work for equality and my dreams for socialism were crushed and came tumbling down. My knees felt like sand and the earthquake beneath my feet trembled endlessly.

At the same time, Morty was his usual detached and depressed self. To add to this pain and chaos, he did not know how to respond to me. He was shocked by my reaction to the loss of my home and life in Levittown and offered to go back, but by then, I knew I could not go back. Not to Levittown or to what had been a depriving relationship. I could not even look at Morty. He apologized, but it was of no use. I had to find a new path.

Gone were the days when Vivian and her children, Freddy and Teddy, would meet my children and me for Saturday lunch and then go off for the afternoon. All of us packed in the car, with no particular destination. We were just out seeking adventure. I was enamored with this great way to discover the rural beauty of Eastern Long Island and its many different landscapes.

The idea came from the play, *The Importance of Being Ernest* by Oscar Wilde, the 19th Century humorist. In the story, Ernest invents a sick friend called "Bunbury", who lives in the countryside and must be attended to from time to time. By so doing, he was able to get a needed rest from his marriage and go off for an escapade — what Oscar Wilde called "bunburying". The story so intrigued me that it became a life long practice of mine. I still go off for these spontaneous trips, although I have no need to invent an invalid friend to explain my carefree getaways. Friends and family are not surprised when I am not to be found for days at a time.

And now here in Franklin Square all these joys were gone. Also gone were the days when we would drop off our kids at one another's homes so we could go off to have free time for ourselves. We were truly an extended family. Then suddenly everything fell apart.

At this moment, my nephew Freddy, who was an honor student in his senior year at McArthur High School in Levittown, was about to take his place in the first class to graduate from this newly built school. Freddy was well known in the community as the editor of the high school newspaper and very involved with the academic life of the school. As the eldest of all our children, Freddy would also be the first to ever go to college. On top of this, there were multiple pressures on him. His father insisted that he graduate at the top of his class. The new high school administration echoed this sentiment because Freddy's high achievements would give the school great prestige in the State. As a result of his accomplishments he was invited to Albany along with a few other high achieving students to be honored by the governor. Although I couldn't stand this incompetent governor, I still have the newspaper photo of Freddy standing besides him, happy and proud.

But all this pressure proved to be more than he could handle. Freddy had a nervous breakdown and was hospitalized at Pilgrim State. While hospitalized, Freddy developed pneumonia and contracted a staph infection. With his weakened immune system mixed with no will to live, Freddy died a month later. His sudden death at seventeen came only months after our move and my emotional breakdown. I know anyone reading of this tragedy in a novel would dismiss it as a gross exaggeration. Nevertheless this was our life.

My children and I lost more than our community and friends. We now lost our Freddy, who, along with Teddy, was like a brother to my daughters. Recovering from one blow after another took many years and on some level, I never truly became whole again. I withdrew completely and home life was dismal for my children, my husband and me.

My extended Levittown family was reeling with pain and disbelief. My father, still living in the Bronx, after many years of happiness with his wife Sylvia and his children's prosperity, returned to the man I remembered him to be during the Depression years. He became sad and withdrawn. Life was difficult for all of us and we just plodded along the best we could. But the impact of Freddy's death caused our close extended family to implode and fall apart.

I remember how we all just lived. The pain was so great and we never spoke about it. We just existed.

A turning point for me came one day, when I was lying in bed, as I often did to cope with my depression during that time. I overheard Morty speaking on the phone to a long-time friend and "comrade" in the communist cause. Morty was complaining to his friend that "Lucille had disgraced the movement by not living up to her commitment." I jumped out of bed in a rage, and the years of frustration came pouring out. I just cried and screamed at him in my defense. Morty left for his sister Jean's house, also on Long Island, where she and her husband, Irving, offered Morty guidance. Irving was a social worker who referred us to his colleague, Mrs. Mitchell, a clinical social worker, for counseling. Morty and I both consulted with her and we each entered individual treatment.

For my sake and the sake of my family, I had to heal the wounds of the many profound losses in my life. I went to therapy two times per week with Mrs. Mitchell, who patiently and empathetically helped me gain more confidence. With the lift of my depression, I was energized and motivated to return to school for my GED. It was then that I found my job at Hillside Hospital. While my commitment to serve people had lain dormant in the recesses of my mind, it was there — ready and finally eager to surface again. Fortunately it did.

I had come to understand that my passion to serve was the engine I needed to achieve a successful life. Not everyone is fortunate enough to find such a focused purpose. As I mentioned earlier, I found mine when, as a young adolescent, I made a pledge to serve and help people. Improving conditions for individuals and society, as a whole, was the principle guiding me through all the years ahead.

This desire and vow to serve took on a new focus. I committed myself to work for the mentally ill. It came to me the very moment I walked in the front door of Hillside Hospital in Queens. Dr. Robins, who had been trained at the Menninger Clinic, ran Hillside Hospital. He introduced Milieu therapy, which is a way of simulating a "normal" life while inside a controlled environment, such as a hospital. The unit becomes the family and the hospital activities outside the unit provide an opportunity for the patients to gain perspective on their interpersonal relationships. Behavioral issues are addressed and worked on at the same time as deeper issues of the psyche are treated in talk therapy. Deeply impressed, I became a volunteer, teaching a class on the United Nations to the patients for two hours a week. The social worker that supervised me, found my work commendable, and with her recommendation I was hired for a paid position as a recreation therapist. Within the hospital setting, using the philosophy of Milieu therapy, the recreation therapist provided an activity in a safe, non-competitive group setting.

If there is ever a Cinderella story in my life this surely is it. No one had ever before been able to enter the professional level at Hillside Hospital without a

Masters degree in Social Work or a related field, and here I was, the exception to the rule. Their trust in me was well deserved. I was dedicated. I could relate to the patients. I brought enthusiasm to everything I did — playing baseball, sewing, painting, sculpting, beading — you name it. I was there to fill the bill and loved every minute working on this large, beautiful hospital campus.

It reminded me of the early days in Elmira — rolling hills and open spaces, walking in the park with the patients, and laughing and running with the wind in my hair as we played ball. I was introduced to ping-pong and loved it. No shooting of a gun allowed, of course. I had to settle for something less threatening, so ping-pong now became my sport of choice.

At this time in the early 1960's, The Ford Foundation was giving college scholarships to mature adults who had life experiences that were equivalent to course work. Experiences such as my work as a recreation therapist at a prestigious hospital, my community organizing and leadership positions, and even my experiences as a mother considered relevant towards college credits. I applied, along with thousands of other applicants, and was among very few who received a scholarship.

I was thrilled to go to Brooklyn College two days a week and was in heaven while I was on the hospital campus. But home life was another matter. While I cooked and cleaned and tried to give my children what they required, I still could not look at my husband.

Unfortunately, in those years, I had not yet learned how to process my tremendous emotional pain, which had a great impact on my relationships with my three daughters. It took years of therapy to learn how to talk things over with others. My early experience as a child had been one in which nothing was ever talked about. It was an unwritten family rule.

Just how strong this family rule was can be seen in the way my mother's death was handled. I was eight years old when my mother, who had just given birth to Raymond, walked out the front door one Friday evening, after saying her prayers over the lit candles. Shortly after, my father and a policeman appeared. My aunts came and rushed my brother and me away in a taxi. My mother was never to be seen or talked about again. I spent years obsessing about what had become of her.

Five years later I found a newspaper clipping in my Aunt Gussie's drawer with an article stating that my mother had walked up to the roof of our apartment building and thrown herself over the ledge. I took the article with me to school to show my best friend. When I returned home, my aunt accused me of taking it and asked for it back. I gave it to her and the incident was never mentioned again, ever. Whatever my mother did was shameful, and I knew I was not to speak about it. I had always felt the shame of her disappearance and it remained buried deep inside me. At thirteen years old it was confirmed. Her act had shocked and embarrassed the whole family. I can still feel a chill and nausea when I think back to that day. I remember going to school in a complete fog. At the end of the school term I was left back. No one in my family seemed to notice my depression and my failure in school.

When I was fifteen years old my Aunt Frieda jumped out of the window of her apartment and killed herself. After learning just two years earlier that my mother had also died from suicide, I now found myself trying to cope with the realization that my mother and my Aunt Frieda, an important mother figure, were both suffering from such despair that they found suicide the only answer. For my own survival I had to shut down emotionally.

Finally, at seventeen I was able to confront my father. I boldly said, "I had a mother, she is dead but she did exist and I want to hear about her." My father could never open up and so I never learned anything about my mother. The only evidence of her existence are a few photos, one on the day of her marriage and a family portrait with me as an infant sitting on my father's lap.

Another illustration of how my father was never able to speak honestly to his children happened when I was pregnant with Jane. My father suddenly announced to Raymond and me that he was taking us out for lunch on the following Saturday. While we were on the train going to Manhattan, my father went to the subway car door at the 170th Street stop and as the doors opened in walked Sylvia, one of my father's friends. We welcomed her and on we went to 34th Street. They walked ahead of us and when they stopped at a men's clothing store she pointed to a suit in the window. I gasped and said to Raymond, "That woman is going to marry our father."

We spent a very pleasant day with our future stepmother. Without a word they were married a few weeks later. Nothing was ever said and we did not attend the wedding. In those days adult children just did not go to a wedding of their parent's second marriages. We did celebrate the occasion sometime later at one of my father's favorite Hungarian restaurants in the Yorkville section of Manhattan. Unfortunately, his inability to communicate established a strong and unhealthy pattern in all of his children, and hurt every one of us as we mirrored this with our loved ones. This explains my behavior with my children and all those around me. Here I must pause to beg their forgiveness.

While getting my degree at Brooklyn College and with my small salary from Hillside Hospital, I was coming to the conclusion that divorce was the only solution to my unhappiness. When I presented my dilemma to my family I received little support, and downright anger from my father. It was the first and only time in my life that I saw such a vehement reaction on his part to anything I did. My sister Vivian's only advice was to "accept my fate" and remain in this unhappy marriage.

My final decision to get a divorce happened suddenly. Early one morning, Morty announced to me that he was withdrawing money from our bank account. In disbelief, I said "But that's the money my father gave me for my college education." After dressing, I grabbed my keys and purse and in a rage ran out of the house, called my friend Edith, and drove to her home in Connecticut. Once there, without thought and still raging inside, I picked up the phone, dialed Morty and told him I wanted a divorce. Morty passively resigned himself to this decision. I acted without planning and moved ahead impulsively. The separation went smoothly and I found that life without Morty seemed to change nothing. He, like my father before him, was never there anyway. Funny, the only difference I experienced was now I had to put the garbage cans out to the curb myself. While we were married I paid the bills, cleaned and cooked, and took care of our children's needs. I did everything, while Morty complained about my going to school and looked at me with distain.

After Morty moved out he contributed $100 a month for child support. At that time Jane was sixteen, Laurie thirteen, and Tami eleven. Combined with my modest salary this was hardly enough to meet our financial demands. Obviously, we had to live on a very tight budget counting every penny and I never knew how I would pay the bills from month to month. Eventually, I decided to sell our house in Franklin Square. One reason for this decision was that Jane wanted to study interior design at the Fashion Institute of Technology in Manhattan. By selling the house we could move to the city and Jane could use public transportation to get to school. Hopefully, we would have some cash in the bank to help us live.

I should have asked for some financial help from my family, but did not. As yet, I had not become "street wise" and without consultation with a bank on refinancing my mortgage, I just went ahead and sold our home in Franklin Square. We moved to a small rental apartment in Flushing. If there is anything to be gained from reading of my life experiences it is that divorce counseling is imperative before any action is taken. As a result of my failure to plan, this period was even more painful than it needed to be. My daughters and I were not used to city life and they had to struggle with the extremely large and over crowed high school, a small apartment and limited financial resources. Jane, Laurie and Tami were battered around and I am afraid I never did explain to them why all this was happening.

I continued to work at Hillside Hospital and persevered with my studies at Brooklyn College. As for the children, what they experienced I do not know. To this day they have not shared all the pain it caused them. But it showed in Jane's distancing herself from me in the years ahead.

Ruben to the rescue — I thought. I met him at a singles weekend shortly after our move to Flushing. Within hours of our meeting this charming and gallant man asked me to marry him. The impulsiveness and tenaciousness of his pursuit should have been a red flag but after a whirlwind romantic courtship of a few months, I agreed.

Ruben was a tall, dark and rugged looking man who had a commanding and self-confident presence. He had all the attributes I associated with the perfect partner, a real Hollywood superman. In fact, my "knight in shining armor" was a brilliant actor who concealed his negative behavior from me and promised me the world. And I was vulnerable to his seductive offer. He had just invented a machine that revolutionized the method of printing on round bottles and he had suddenly become extremely wealthy. Ruben had a factory in Kearny, New Jersey and he seemed like a creative and honest businessman. He offered to pay for my education, which meant I would not have to work and go to school at the same time. After we married Ruben bought a home for us and we moved into a grand mansion on Ridgewood Avenue in Glen Ridge, New Jersey. The house cost $34,000 in 1965, and is now worth well over two million.

All my life I longed to live in "a place that was good to come from" and I finally had it. Ridgewood Avenue was the most distinguished block in one of the most prestigious towns in all of New Jersey. We moved into a brilliantly landscaped home during the peak of summer. The gardens along Ridgewood Avenue were magical. Each one of us had our own spacious bedroom with a private bathroom. Hattie was hired as our housekeeper. Within days, though, Ruben's paranoid and angry nature emerged and he complained about everything my children did, becoming increasingly sullen and withdrawn. My children began to walk on eggshells when he was around. Within a short time, they hid in their rooms when he appeared at the front door. They each reacted to this situation in their own way. Jane opted out for an apartment in Manhattan. Tami wasn't around long either. It was too stodgy and upper class for her growing political consciousness. She quit high school in the tenth grade and was off to live in a commune on the Lower East Side. Laurie, on the other hand, loved the small town atmosphere of Glen Ridge High School and developed many friends in the community, but she sure disliked Ruben.

What I later began to understand was that Ruben had a paranoid personality disorder, which explains his pervasive jealousy and his vigilant need for control. Within a month he stopped supporting me. The bills kept coming and we had many collectors at our doorstep. No money. No Ruben. I panicked. What was to become of me? I had given up my job at Hillside Hospital to marry and move to New Jersey. With no diploma, where would I get a job?

I had developed a close relationship with Hattie and luckily she was there to guide me. She'd had a life of struggle as an African American single mother and, in her own words, had become "street-wise." With Hattie leading the way, I hired a lawyer and pursued a separation agreement. The only lawyer I had known was a union lawyer who did not understand how to handle tough divorce negotiations. Eventually, I dropped him and found a divorce lawyer, reputed to be a mean negotiator. Hattie advised me to go to an accountant who taught me how to plan my finances for the years ahead. By that time, I had almost completed all my courses for my undergraduate degree. But, I realized I still had much more to learn about life before I could claim I had completed my education. Another divorce, a signed agreement giving me eighty-five dollars a week and papers informing me to vacate the house on Ridgewood Avenue — I was on my own again. I had become "street-wise" but money was still a huge problem. I promised myself I would never again make a move without the advice of a lawyer, an accountant and even a psychiatrist.

We moved to Union City, New Jersey where we found a great and very cheap apartment in the home of an Italian family. Our monthly rent was $135 with no increases for the entire five years I lived there. Tami moved back to live with Laurie and me, and we all crammed into this small apartment that overlooked the Hudson River, set high on a cliff. At night the New York skyline glittered brighter than I ever imagined it could. There we were, on top of the Palisades, with an in-ground swimming pool nestled into this magical Italian villa style house. Alas, at this time I must admit Union City was not "a place that was good to come from." My sociology professor told me so, and he should know about these matters. In fact, Union City was celebrated for its brothels and saloons.

Union City had the charm of a small village in Italy. The vendors would shout out their vegetables for sale, the fish was openly displayed on carts, and of course, the fresh fruit was colorfully presented. Broken English was spoken and everyone welcomed me. A few people even offered their help in finding me a good man.

Time does not stand still as I am reminded of frequently, and time did move on along with changes on Bergenline Avenue. The Spanish language became mixed with Italian as more and more Cubans made Union City their home. Evenings could be spent eating at home-style Italian or Cuban restaurants. I even took one of my dates to a saloon, now called a bar, which had the flavor of bygone days. Imagine my shock when a stripper appeared not twelve feet from where we were seated.

An architect from Italy built the white stucco villa we now lived in. This house was his attempt to replicate his very own home in the Old Country. After he died, the family divided the house into apartments and his wife, Nonnie, and their sons, Gulio and Tony, lived in their own apartments with their families. If Gulio came to visit us in our apartment Tony was sure to follow. The environment was warm and embracing. I remember the response of an old, wealthy friend who had once visited me in Levittown and was now visiting me in Union City. He told me how unusual it was that in Union City, as in Levittown, we could just ask a neighbor for some milk. The experience years ago in Levittown seemed to have so impressed him that he could still recall the event. He commented that in his upscale neighborhood this would never happen. So much for my aunts' wish for me! I now had *my* American Dream.

I expanded my professional life by working as the director of a cerebral palsy center and it was during this time that I made the decision to go to social work school. Still insecure and a little nervous, I called Gary Rosenberg, who I had known at Hillside Hospital, and who was now the Dean of Admissions at Adelphi School of Social Work. I remember the exact words I used, "Gary, I want to be a social worker." He was responsive and encouraged me to come out to Garden City. I then said, "Gary, I don't have money." His response to every one of my concerns was met with an enthusiastic positive rejoinder. Yes, he would help me apply for a scholarship, and yes, he would get me a car. His support was very much needed at this time in my life and I was overwhelmed by such an appreciation of my professional ability. I waited for another year and with his help, I received a National Mental Health grant, a full scholarship, and my housing expenses were paid as well. I was not only admitted, I was given the red carpet to Adelphi School of Social Work.

These Union City years were also filled with many

men friends. I tell of my experiences with great pleasure. I had learned to enjoy men's attention without getting overly involved and welcomed many men into my life — some as platonic friends, and others as lovers.

This was the time of the sexual revolution and people were seriously questioning the institution of marriage and monogamy. And I was liberated enough to enjoy multiple relationships simultaneously.

For five years I was truly in love with Ira, but he was married. While he had been a great lover, he would have been a terrible husband. On the other hand, Sal would have been a good husband, but I did not love him. He was fun and even drove thirty miles to buy me a twenty-five cent Italian ice, which he claimed was the best in New Jersey, but the chemistry wasn't there for me. Costas remained in my life for many years and was always there to comfort me in my many difficult moments. He truly loved me but marriage to him was out of the question. Although he was twenty years younger than I, with his "old country" Greek ways, he seemed twenty years older. There was the editor of a scientific monthly and the professor of English who tried to help me write, and I surely fell for the Marxist but he was too ethereal and other worldly. I remember George, the minister, for his

78

majestic appearance, but dear me, he was just too earthbound.

Then there was Sam. There was so much about him that I loved. He was brilliant, fun loving and always had new exciting things to do. He taught me everything I ever wanted to know about cockroaches and I was impressed. But there again was the "but"... he was not good looking. Could my aunt's judgmental scorn be rearing its head?

One Christmas, I invited the whole family for dinner at my Union City apartment. Sam helped me prepare the meal. The afternoon was full of fun and good humor. When everyone had gone and I was alone with my father, he said in his Jewish sing song manner, "And how about Sam?" I knew what he meant and I responded, "Poppa, he's too fat." To which my father replied, "So, what's fat?" On it went. "Poppa, he has no hair." "So what's hair?" After a few more rounds I laughed and said, "Poppa, you're desperate for me to marry aren't you?"

A few months after this incident, I learned of Sam's marriage to one of the most prominent psychotherapists in New York City. I realize now, with my distorted values, I was still looking for a Hollywood superman that would meet the approval of my judgemental aunts.

While I was living in Union City, I began to explore the world beyond the United States. My first trip was a two-week vacation in Italy. The following year, I plopped down my five hundred dollars and traveled to Ireland. All my adventures over the years were memorable but the most important one was when I traveled to Mexico with my daughter Tami and her friend Heather. At the young age of nineteen, Tami was already a natural leader. She had left the United States in 1968 to study in Mexico and Cuba.

In the spring of 1970, I was planning to begin my second year of Social Work School in the fall, still unsure if my grant would come through. Tami had received a small grant to make a documentary about the political situation in Central America. I was sitting on her bed while she and Heather laid out the plans for their project. Seeing the sadness on my face, she suddenly turned to me and said, "Ma, buy a back pack and come with us." I gasped. What about the summer job I had found to tide me over? What about money? Just as with Gary Rosenberg, Tami's response was an enthusiastic, "We'll find money." Of course I would go, and in no more than a few weeks we were on our way.

Tami taught me how to go beyond first impressions while traveling in a foreign country and dig deeper into the political and social conditions existing at the time. On some level the experience changed my life. I fell in love with Mexico and its people. It expanded my horizons to incorporate Latin America into my ever-growing list of social concerns.

Under Tami's commanding guidance, I obeyed her every instruction. Get up, sit down, eat and shower whenever you can for you never know when there will be another opportunity to do so. We hitchhiked from one town to another as she and Heather sought new arenas to film. On some occasions I was left behind while the camera had to be taken to Mexico City for repairs or when they traveled to Guatemala without me. Everything was basic, the lodgings, the vehicles we rode in, and of course, the camera. My love of adventure soared when Tami, her work completed in a particular location, would announce, "We move tomorrow, first thing in the morning." With the sun breaking on the horizon, we were off to a new challenge.

When we arrived at a new town, housing was always the first thing on the agenda. Tami and Heather would find a convent or a person they knew from past trips. We simply had no money to spend on lodging. General Mujica's widow's home was luxurious. Maria's shack, which she shared with her son, her father, and their animals, was equally welcoming. I had a hard time containing my excitement. With Tami's tutelage I searched for the true essence of the culture and was introduced to the revolutionary works of the great muralists of Mexico. They were all monumental, scathing in their political statements. Jose Clemente Orozco's work from the 1930's was riveting and I instantly became his follower. I searched throughout Mexico to see all of his masterpieces. In Guadalajara I lay on the floor looking skyward to see Orozco's mural, gasping with disbelief as I viewed the simple, dynamic figures in rich native colors strongly influenced by Mexican Indian traditions. I had been dazzled by Michelangelo's murals in the Sistine Chapel, and here again, by another artist, so different, so magnificent, representing an Indian culture. After my return to New York I traveled to New Hampshire to the Baker Library at Dartmouth College to see Orozco's fresco, Modern Migration of the Spirit. He created a panorama of the history of the America's, which climaxes in a great, flayed figure of Christ destroying his own cross. Because his was an art of social protest, Orozco had such appeal to Americans concerned with human dignity and justice, like myself.

My scholarship came through and I returned to the states after one of the most exciting experiences of my life. After completing two years of social work school, with my MSW degree in hand, I was ready to go to work. Unfortunately, when I graduated in 1971 the job market was flat and I was offered only entry-level positions. After my years of struggling through school and my many experiences working with Milieu therapy, I was not ready to change course and accept an entry-level position. Finally, I was offered a job as the Director of After Care in a clinic serving Creedmore State Mental Hospital's former patients who were being integrated into community life in Far Rockaway. This new and exciting approach of integrating the mentally ill into the community was being implemented throughout the state. I grabbed it immediately, although I was able to postpone the starting day because I had another opportunity to travel.

My brother Arthur invited me to travel with him and his wife to one of his homes as his gift to me for completing graduate school. At first I didn't want to accept because of our difficult and often contentious relationship. Arthur and I were as different as two people could be; he - conventional and status driven, me - bohemian and socially conscious. The scars of an unloving and disruptive childhood had an impact on Arthur that I never fully understood while he was alive.

I simply saw him as a self-centered man who ran with the wealthy-privileged of Washington D.C., never comfortable inside his Jewish body. It took me years to understand why. He had been raised for much of his life by our three aunts and was profoundly influenced by their values.

My aunts and mother were deeply affected by the anti-Semitism that permeated Hungary during their youth. In order to get an education they had to attend Christian schools. Shortly after arriving in the United States, in the early 1900's, Gussie, Frieda and Regina converted to the Church of Christian Scientists. When my mother arrived here with her sisters she found herself settled in a bustling Jewish community in New York City. She must have been moved and inspired by the open observance of Jewish traditions. My mother found enough support and strength in this community to reject the negative impact from the past and chose to embrace her Judaism. In order to practice her religion she consciously set about to learn some of the prayers and rituals of Jewish life.

With the breakup of our family after her death, Arthur ended up living with our aunts and inherited their discomfort with being Jewish. Years later when Jane was a teenager she stayed with Arthur for the summer. When she arrived at his home, Arthur had

Jane remove her necklace with a small gold Star of David discreetly hanging from her neck. What amazes me still is how the anti-Semitism of the late 1800's continued in my family and imposed itself on the third generation.

Arthur never thanked the aunts for the home he had with them as a child; the college education they paid for and the strings they pulled to get him his first job at a time when Jews were not hired in the field of engineering. Funny, though they converted to Christianity they would have to pull strings to get their "Jewish" nephew a job.

The lives of Aunts Regina and Gussie ended in poverty having first been bankrupted by the stock market crash of 1929 and then, after much renewed business success, they made poor business decisions and had little saved for retirement. Arthur died in 1985 with his money hidden, finally recovered by his only daughter after a long litigation.

Eventually my friends convinced me that I needed a vacation before starting my new job. I accepted Arthur's invitation and went from rags to riches for five weeks while visiting him in Costa del Sol, Spain. We traveled from one five-star hotel to another, quite a contrast from my time in Mexico. We never really hung out with the people of Spain. At night we ate at exclusive restaurants and I rubbed elbows, so I was told, with the elite. I escaped from time to time. Once to the brilliant museums of Madrid and then again, before I left Spain, to vibrant Barcelona where I really learned to dance.

Back in the states I was ready to begin my new life. After five happy years in Union City, my children out of the house, my Masters of Social Work degree in hand, I moved to Far Rockaway to become the director of an aftercare center for psychiatric patients who had been discharged from the hospital.

3

My 'Renaissance'

So what if Far Rockaway was no better a place to come from than Union City. Who cared? I had reached my educational goal. It took me ten years to get my undergraduate degree and then my master's and I was eager to start an aftercare program affiliated with Creedmore State Mental Hospital. With my exposure to the theory of Milieu therapy during my years at Hillside, I was prepared to initiate an innovative program.

Not yet three days on the job, I received a call from Morris Weinberg, the Director of the Educational Alliance. He was the head of one of the most prestigious centers in the state, which continues to serve the Lower East Side community of New York City. Without any small talk he offered me the

Directorship of the Adult Program at the Educational Alliance. I didn't hesitate for a moment and turned it down — the big salary, the benefits, and great prestige that went with the position. After a short goodbye, still stunned, I got off my chair, walked down the hall to the office of the center's director of my new job, knocked, entered and said in a flat voice, "Tony, I just turned down an offer to be the Director of the Adult Program at the Educational Alliance." Without another word, I turned around and went back to my desk.

I had made a pledge to revolutionize treatment for the mentally ill and I would not change course now, not even for a prestigious job at the Educational Alliance. The Aftercare Program was initiated with a small but enthusiastic staff. As we began to set it in motion, we worked closely with the patients about to be discharged from Creedmoor State Mental Hospital, and encouraged them to join our program. We reassured these bewildered and frightened "inmates", as they were called, and promised that we would be there for them every step of the way.

One of the challenges for me as the Director was to train my staff in this new method, with its unique approach of working with the mentally disturbed. It included individual psychotherapy, group therapy, art and movement therapy and vocational training. The founding principle of this treatment was to create an environment where people would leave the hospital and be integrated into community life. In addition, I was expected to treat mentally ill patients already living in the community.

Mental illness was not new to me. My mother and my aunt Frieda had committed suicide due to major depressive disorders. My nephew Freddy had been hospitalized when he had a psychological breakdown. And aunt Regina had been hospitalized throughout my childhood. I remember her as being smart, dynamic and witty. She suffered from severe paranoia and we would often find handwritten notes stabbed into the walls with a knife. The content of these notes were always the same. A Jewish man was following her and threatening her life. I remember when we first realized she was the author of these notes. Finally, in 1951 Regina was institutionalized at Pilgrim State Hospital until the end of her life. Shortly before she died Regina confessed to me that she had been mistaken. The man following her was not Jewish after all, he was Christian. I understood mental illness personally and profoundly.

One of my clients already living in the community was Robert, a white nineteen year-old outpatient who was diagnosed as a schizophrenic. The report given to me emphasized that he functioned fairly well in the community. I was assigned to work with him on a one-on-one basis creating a supportive and warm environment. While he was in treatment with me, my car was vandalized numerous times. During one instance, my tires were stolen and the car parked next to mine was burnt down to the ground. Despite all of my official complaints to the police, they dismissed these acts as just random hoodlum activity. Eventually, I was forced to move to a quiet community nearby but my car was vandalized yet again. Again, I went to the police and finally they took me seriously. They asked me to supply them with a list of young men in treatment at the clinic. Within one hour the police identified Robert as the suspect. He had been picked up frequently for loitering at an elementary school. I was amazed to learn that I had no legal recourse. I could not have him arrested and the state would not hospitalize him.

The laws were changing in New York State and the new official policy was to release patients out of the hospitals into the communities. They began this approach prematurely, without a serious infrastructure in place. In addition, the clinic's response was that this was my problem not theirs. Months later, at a party, I was told in a flippant manner by a psychologist, that Robert had killed himself. He went on to say, "Lucille, it was you or him." My stomach turned from both fear and my pain for Robert. Though this was a difficult experience, I did not run away from the profession.

I remember sitting at my desk when Frank, a day client, walked in and stated, "I think I killed my girlfriend." I suggested that he have a seat and tell me more. He explained that he tied a noose around his girlfriend's neck and left her for dead. I was the first person he reported this to. I thanked him. Reaching for my phone while Frank was still speaking, I called a colleague and told him to join me on a home visit.

It was a dismal, rainy and unusually eerie day. The three of us entered this isolated community of abandoned small houses in Far Rockaway where many of the poor were living as squatters. Frank pointed to the house where he and his girlfriend were living. We pushed opened the dilapidated white picket gate and entered cautiously as Frank called out, "Marie, Marie!" I noticed a head of hair hanging over a bed and walked, very slowly, towards it and gently touched Marie's body and asked, "Marie, can you hear me?" She responded with a very soft "Yes." Hearing this, my client angrily screamed, "Marie, you didn't lift your head high enough so that I could get the noose around your head!" When the situation calmed down, I suggested to Marie that we call the police and that she have him arrested. I explained to her that legally she had to place the complaint. Marie basically said "no thank you." I never saw them again.

The state was emptying hospitals of the mentally ill without providing my program, or for that matter any program, with enough staff and space and supervised housing to make possible any success in supportive reentry into communities. Little did I know at the time that New York State would only implement the first part of this new statewide program, emptying hospitals of the mentally ill. The state then failed to fund the second part, providing aftercare for those pushed out of hospitals. New York State lacked the commitment to serve and rehabilitate the mentally ill, which prevented me from putting my education and the techniques of Milieu therapy into full use. At this point in my career, I was not naive about the difficulty and sometimes impossibility of rehabilitating the seriously mentally ill. However, if we were committed to discharge patients from the hospitals, we would have to create a supportive environment with on-going supervision, training, psychotherapy and medication. On top of

(L-R) Lucille's family
Mother, sister Vivian, brother Arthur, father & Lucille on father's lap (1921)

Lucille's maternal
grandparents

Lucille at age 14 with her brother Raymond, 7 (1934)

Lucille and Morty (1942)

Lucille in Elmira, NY (1942)

Lucille working in factory in Syracuse, NY

Photo taken by Lucille in Mississippi (1943)

*Lucille with nephew Teddy,
Levittown, NY (1949)*

*(L-R) Tami, Lucille & Laurie in
Levittown, NY*

(L-R) Jane, friends, with cousins Freddy & Teddy, Levittown, NY

Starr Koss Rickma

Family in Levittown with Aunt Gussie in the center (1961)

(L-R) Tami, Laurie, Lucille & Jane (1984)

*Grandaughters at Pro Choice demonstration in Washington, DC with Tami
(1992)*

Lucille's grandchildren and grand nieces (2000)

Lucille at Hillside Hospital

Hitch hiking in Mexico (1970)

Leaving for Mexico. Backpacking with Tami and Heather (1970)

(L-R) Raymond, Vivian, Lucille, Max, Sylvia & Arthur at fathers 80th Birthday (1968)

Mr Puppy

Lucille, extreme right, with extended family (1995)

LIFT THE EMBARGO AGAINST THE SPANISH REPUBLIC

For the Honor and Defense of Democracy—

Strike off the embargo chains on the Spanish Republic.

"that the government of the people, by the people, and for the people shall not perish from the earth."

All America is Aroused

Hitler, Mussolini and Franco are slaughtering thousands of innocent women and children with devastating air bombardments.

Franco openly boasts that he will blow 105 unarmed towns and villages of the Spanish Republic off the map. Already thousands of civilians have been killed and injured.

America can make it possible for the Spanish people to defend themselves by purchasing anti-aircraft guns and munitions here. *Americans who fought for and won their own republic can give the Spanish people the chance to protect and preserve their republic.*

By lifting the embargo *NOW*, America can help prevent the victory of fascism in Spain and its spread to the Spanish-speaking democracies of Latin America.

All America Must Act Now!

- Send a personal message to President Roosevelt telling him you want the embargo lifted;
- Ask your organization to write the President;
- Initiate and take part in conferences and mass meetings called for this purpose;
- Write letters to newspaper editors, telephone your friends, visit your Congressmen and Senators letting them know how you feel on this subject;
- Support the NATIONAL "LIFT THE EMBARGO" CONFERENCE IN WASHINGTON, D. C., ON MONDAY, JANUARY 9th, by sending delegates from your organization or community.

FRIENDS OF THE ABRAHAM LINCOLN BRIGADE
125 WEST 45th STREET
NEW YORK, N. Y.

 204

Self-Portrait by Author

this, there was always the concern for the safety of the communities they were reentering into. As a profession, we could not facilitate this huge task without the economic commitment from the government.

My experiences as a director of an after care program for the mentally ill foreshadowed the disastrous and dangerous societal condition that was to come. This was the moment in the mid 1970's when our society could have made a different decision. I witnessed the birth of what later became known as the Homeless Population, a population that we now take for granted on the streets of many cities across this country.

After many more frustrations at the Far Rockaway clinic I reluctantly came to understand that I could no longer work there. In a farewell luncheon the Director, Tony, gave me a gift – the moving book *Jonathan Livingston Seagull* by Richard Bach. This was Tony's way of acknowledging that, like the courageous seagull in the book, I was always reaching beyond the status quo —trying to achieve new heights and possibilities.

Shortly thereafter, I was hired by Brooklyn State Hospital to run an aftercare program located in a YMCA. Again, I started with great enthusiasm and hired Terry, an energetic and forward thinking new graduate from Fordham University as my assistant, only to realize, within weeks, that we were dealing with complacent state workers who had become cynical in the government bureaucracy. They were protected by a strong union, and would do things their way and at their convenience. The union only saw the needs of the workers it represented and this came into conflict with my need to get the job done. Ironically, having been a union organizer much of my life, I now found myself at odds with a union, which I thought was losing its mission. Ultimately, I was the one to scrub floors and carry equipment. The program progressed but with summer upon us the basement became unbearably hot and the other rooms available to us were much too cold. I tried to work with the Director of the YMCA but he stood firm, saying this was what the contract called for.

Finally, my frustration grew too great, and I impulsively blurted out that we would leave the YMCA and go elsewhere when the state contract expired. It took only three days for me to receive a call from Dr. Cane, the Director of Social Services at Brooklyn State Hospital, ordering me back to the hospital. When I arrived I found the Director pacing the floor. Seeing me he exploded, "You may be a great clinician but you sure…" His words trailed off in a grumble. Dr. Cane sat me down and told me he had received a phone call from the governor himself about the threat I had made. The Director of the YMCA just happened to be the brother of the governor's assistant. If the YMCA lost the contract with the hospital they would lose the huge rental income they received from New York State. Dr. Cane was right. Though I could see these injustices, I didn't know how to negotiate and compromise within a bureaucratic system.

The final decision to leave Brooklyn State Hospital came when my assistant was assailed by one of our clients, who attempted to strangle her with a wire hanger. We saved Terry's life, but understandably, she quit the very next day. In her farewell letter to me she lamented, "You are a great general, but without an army you just can't achieve your goals. Think about it."

Years later I saw the play *Man of La Mancha* and smiled to myself. I, too, was dreaming the impossible dream. *Man of La Mancha* was a popular play on Broadway based on the story written by Cervantes, a 16th century Spanish author who wrote the novel Don Quixote. Don Quixote "dreamed the impossible dream" and was an idealist visionary who I have identified with through out my life.

I stayed on, pleading for a guard to be assigned to our facility. When the request was refused I went job hunting. Although I was a strong "general", it took many years of additional schooling in social work organization and administration to learn to be less idealistic, to compromise with administrators and deepen my mediation skills.

Far Rockaway was a wonderful place to live. In the middle of this urban sprawl, just blocks from the subway, was the ocean where I spent many an afternoon swimming, sunning and walking on the beach. My social life expanded when I was invited to participate in a Consciousness Raising Group (CR) for single women organized by the National Organization of Women. The group ranged in age from twenty-six to sixty-two. Each week a new topic was chosen and we round-robined it, never reacting but learning from one another's experiences. Soon after this group was formed we realized we had found a new very special family.

One of the most dramatic discussions was on money management. We all failed miserably in this area and were surprised by our lack of knowledge in the fundamentals of financial matters. It is no wonder we immediately called a special luncheon where we assigned each participant the responsibility of finding out about interest rates at banks and other financial institutions.

Another discussion, this time about sex, caused us to lose three members. Hearing masturbation discussed in descriptive terms was new to most of us, but was particularly disturbing and threatening to the few who left the group. The experience was mind-expanding and at the age of 58, I realized I was still naive. Though I had many wonderful love relationships, I was uncomfortable talking about sex.

Our CR Group developed into a supportive and social network, sharing Sunday dinners and many holidays with our children and men friends. We stood by one of our sister's, Burnett, when her lover died and again we were there for Gert when her son, Phil Ochs, committed suicide. He was a well-known folk singer, and along with the rest of the country, we mourned his shocking and untimely death. The highs and lows we shared brought us closer than ever. I became aware of the larger Women's Movement around us. We read books like *The Feminine Mystique* by Betty Friedan and *Sexual Politics* by Kate Millett, which challenged our preconditioned thoughts of what it was to be a woman. Many of us were able to understand our personal experiences through a different lens, that of a second-class citizen. We were nurturing each other, woman to woman, and at the same time we were realizing that, in fact, out of this new experience we had become intelligent, deep thinking and independent people. None of us were ever the same after that.

The seventies were remarkable times. One weekend, I took five of my CR sisters to Su Casa, my favorite weekend getaway in the Catskills where nudity was celebrated. We were given the attic digs, a large open space with six beds, just right for us. Saturday night I never even made it downstairs, for every time I started to get dressed someone would come to the room and offer me a puff of marijuana and I just settled back and got stoned, spending the weekend in a marijuana fog. Two of my sisters from the CR group found romantic partners — Miriam's Maurice and Sandy's Steve. Sandy and Steve married following a short courtship. After tiring of Maurice, Miriam had a difficult time getting rid of him.

Up until this time, many of my CR sisters had only socialized in couples. Their relationship with each other, as with many women from my generation, was limited to talking about our children and domestic life. The experiences at Su Casa released some of my CR sisters and me to a freer life style that forever reshaped my social life.

The climate that created the revolution in women's identity also prompted radical changes in the mental health professions. My first encounter with this growing revolt took place at a conference held in New York City at the Hilton Hotel. Men in proper dark suits sat lined up at the podium ready to speak. Suddenly, casually dressed men dashed to the front of the conference room and pulled the microphone from the speaker's hand pronouncing, "Freud is dead and so are his Victorian theories!" I remember the spot where I was standing. There I was in my proper beige suit with my mouth wide open wondering what would come next. I was prepared to run at any moment if the situation became volatile.

Right before me, I saw Freud figuratively toppled from his pedestal. I don't know how long it took me to regain my composure but when I did I wandered the streets for some time imagining what was next. A new opportunity opened where I could fully explore unconventional psychological theories and interactive and experiential techniques. Now there was nothing I would not try — T-groups, encounter weekends, EST seminars.

I remember it well, lying on the floor with a man's foot on my stomach daring me to fight back. I cried and ranted along with everyone else and we called it liberating. Then there was the time I took my daughter Laurie to a session at the majestic Riverside Church. We were taken to the tower and told to lie down on the black mats provided for us. When the lights were dimmed the instructor, in a soft voice, directed us to start talking to our mothers. With further encouragement participants began talking, and in a short time the voices got louder, filling the air with great emotion. In time I heard weeping and loud cries. The air was filled with sobbing. Suddenly, I heard a cry above the others, "Ma, let's get out of here." That was Laurie's voice, and we both escaped, laughing all the way.

I participated in Gestalt group experiences, where we pounded chairs with our fists, expressing our anger and frustration, shouting obscenities at our abusers. These were not isolated events. I belonged to two organizations that had regular weekend retreats. In addition, I went to monthly evening meetings held in New York City where presentations were made of new methods being developed by innovative clinicians. It was at one of these meetings where I met Carl Rogers, who taught me humility in working with people, pointing out that clinicians were traveling the road together with our clients working through life's many challenges. Another eminent psychiatrist, Albert Ellis, made a deep impression on me, with his bellowing voice and his gutter language. Inspired by these new interpersonal approaches, I said to a client of mine, who had seven years of traditional therapy, "You keep asking why you do destructive things. You know the answers, just stop doing them." We were both shocked by my sharp intervention but it produced change in our ongoing work together. I studied other pioneering techniques, like hypnosis, which added to my skills as a clinician. Hypnosis was particularly well suited to my interest in combining the newer modalities. It integrates the unconscious process with meditation and visualization.

Rockaway days were my Renaissance days and I loved the excitement of it all, however, having resigned from my job with Brooklyn State Hospital, I was ready to go wherever a new job would take me. I understood that if I had to move to a new community I would be leaving my CR Group. But being a wanderer wasn't new to me and I had learned from my childhood, when I left a community I left every thing behind, friendships included.

My new job brought me to Patchoque in 1975 where I was hired as a supervisor of one of the mental health clinics in Suffolk County, Long Island, run by Catholic Charities. I was eager to begin a new position, and did not even bother to ask for any particulars about my new duties. When I arrived at the center I was shown many offices I could choose from. The administrator suggested that with my position I should select the largest office, set in the center of the building, with a door on both sides of the room. He then left me, saying he would come for me when the staff was assembled. I sat in a leather chair at the auspicious, oversized desk and with my hand holding up my head I muttered out loud, "Lucille, I do believe you are the head of the whole darn thing." This would be a first for me and I was anxious. I met the staff, sitting at the head of a long conference table, wondering how I would pull this off. The next day I visited Tony, the director of my previous job in Far Rockaway, and confessed my dilemma asking for his help. He assigned someone to me and I spent the rest of the day learning the basics of how to be the chief administrator of a mental health center.

Once again, the most important part of my work was to set up an aftercare program for the patients released from Pilgrim State Psychiatric Hospital. Half of the new building had been allotted for that purpose, but the money was never appropriated by the state legislature and the construction work was never completed. My wish to modernize the way services were administered to the mentally ill was thwarted again. I watched as the mentally ill were released from Pilgram State Hospital and were filling the streets of Patchogue and Bayshore, causing havoc with their erratic behavior. The owners of large houses began renting rooms to these people, overcrowding this residential community and overburdening the community's resources. Many of the former psychiatric patients caused disturbances wherever they went. I looked on in dismay as people in the community began to demand something be done with "those terrible people."

It did not take long for those released from the mental hospitals to be jailed for vagrancy and minor criminal activities. The hospitals they were discharged from now remained vacant as new jails were being built to house the displaced and disenfranchised mentally disabled people. Though still an idealist, I understood by this time in my life that the system of capitalism would never commit money to support and serve the mentally ill.

Although the aftercare program was sabotaged by a lack of funds and government commitment, the work in the Catholic Charities program developed, offering therapeutic services to individuals as well as women's groups. The Women's Movement continued to inspire me and I set up groups for abused women, women wanting to get into the work force and women wanting assertiveness training. Catholic Charities programs included services for the emerging ethnic groups as well. Working with the growing Puerto Rican community was new and I remember helping set up self-help groups as well as arranging a two-week camp program for their children. When we learned that the parents would not separate from their children, not even for two-weeks, we changed it to a family camp.

Sister Claire, my assistant, was clever and good humored. After a few months of working together she became one of my best friends and was always doing something to make me laugh. I remember the day she called me on the intercom and alerted me that she needed my help, urgently. When I went to see her, she explained that we had to make a run to the A&P. So off we went to pick up day old bread to be delivered to the migrant workers living in camps at the end of town. Arriving at the service entrance of the supermarket, Sister Claire and I started hauling the bread and while in the process she turned to the store manager and said, " I'd like to introduce you to the director of our clinic, Dr. Gold." The now stunned store manager, who had been watching a director from a prestigious agency haul bread, quickly assigned a clerk to take over the task. Sister Claire always had another prank up her sleeve. Our relationship grew into a warm, intellectual and unique friendship. However, I suddenly became aware of Sister Claire's sexual attraction to me. I even flirted with the idea of responding but realized this wasn't for me and gently moved away from our strong attachment.

There was revolution everywhere, in my profession, among women and in the political arena, and even in the sanctified halls of a convent. I spent many evenings at the convent sharing dinner and conversation with the other nuns. I heard talk of their dissatisfaction with being second-class citizens and having to serve the priests. They wanted to be paid for their work, and contribute to Social Security so they could retire with dignity and security at the end of their service. The nuns were even questioning the role of the Catholic Church itself. Ideas were thrown around — Buddhism, Paganism, even Darwinism. The sisters were exploring all possibilities.

One pivotal experience for me at Catholic Charities was leading a ten-week course for volunteers from Blue Point Parish. The objective of this workshop was for the parish to set up its own social service programs led by these volunteers. My favorite student was Father Buckley. He was the head priest of Blue Point Parish, and had been a professor at St. John's University. He decided to experience life among the parishioners and came down from the Ivy Tower of university life.

Teaching came naturally to me and I loved having Father Buckley in the workshop. I helped to develop a curriculum that included art therapy as one of the techniques used to help participants uncover deeper feelings. The students in this workshop responded enthusiastically and were excited to use these new skills in the communities they were serving.

Father Buckley and I became good friends and when the program was completed he presented me with a thank you note and one of his art works, a dynamic lithograph of Jesus coming down off the cross. I felt he was letting me know something personal, that the obstacle of working within the church was too difficult for him and faced with resistance from the hierarchy, he became more and more frustrated. After a few visits to my office Father Buckley sent me a farewell letter, saying he was leaving his parish because of this bureaucracy. He went back to his position as a professor at St. John's University.

Many dedicated people I met along the way left social services because it is unappreciated work with so many obstacles. Father Buckley, a gentle and generous soul, may not be your typical Hollywood superstar, but he sure was my hero.

My work was gaining national attention when, suddenly, the Executive Director of Catholic Charities, Father Fagin, selected me to become the Education Director for Catholic Charities on Long Island. I would be the first woman director, and I should add, the first Jewish woman ever to reach the top of their hierarchy. There was one caveat, I would have to go to the main office located in Rockville Center. The idea of moving again was unthinkable. This move would mean a loss of my wonderful home base, my assistant Sister Claire, and my beautiful garden apartment. It was just unthinkable. I emphatically said, "No thank you, I love my work in Patchogue." Father Fagin tried repeatedly to change my mind, and many people warned me about the consequences, but I held my ground. I learned too late that the decision of a powerful priest should not be challenged, and sure enough, I was fired and back on the street.

4
My Arrival

I was not offered a job for one solid year. Either I was over-qualified or under-qualified. As a political activist and a community organizer I had never had the professional goal to develop a private practice. But out of necessity I started seeing clients at my home. I used my small dining room in my garden apartment as the treatment room and my colorful antique filled living room as a waiting area, which was also an inviting space for group therapy. I had business cards professionally designed and acquired a telephone service. To improve my visibility I rented a small office in Islip for fifty dollars a month. In this lovely professional space I had an office waiting room, which I shared with two lawyers and their secretaries.

Everyone assumed the secretaries were also there to serve me, an innocuous deception, which served me well indeed. With two offices, one in Patchogue and one in Islip, I impressed the community. Truly on my own for the first time in my life, I was in business and it wasn't long before I was doing quite well. I had a good referral base with the priests in the parishes sending me their troubled parishioners who they were unable to help. They not only sent me people in trouble, but also those who needed annulments that would be honored by the church. I supplied them with the necessary documentation and then they could receive the blessing of the church and be remarried by a Catholic priest.

I became known as a feminist therapist and at the same time, noted for the spirituality I brought to treatment. My practice kept me very busy with individual and group therapy sessions. With money now flowing in I was encouraged by my accountant to invest in a house. After all, I had finally become street wise and learned the tricks of the capitalist system, with its perks and loopholes for the "well heeled."

The purchase of a house would provide me with many tax advantages including the financial benefits of having a home office. And so it was in the fall of 1979,

I moved into my house in Sayville, Long Island, which I chose because I had heard Sayville was "a place that was good to come from."

This classic house absolutely charmed me with its 19th century detail and spacious yard with a large swimming pool. I had arrived — a stimulating and vital private practice, a beautiful Colonial home and a community with easy access to the ocean. But what was most important was that my two conflicting drives were realized. Not only had I achieved financial stability, but I was also playing a productive and proactive role in people's lives, both as a therapist and as the head of the Islip Women's Center. I believed my aunts would finally be pleased with me because I had climbed and climbed and now, at last, I had arrived at their "American Dream."

For me, after Levittown I did not have time for dreams, yet here I was with so much. I decorated my new home with Early American and Victorian furnishings and ornaments I had purchased for so little over the years on my weekend bunburying trips. I also shopped at the Salvation Army in Riverhead and the used furniture outlets along Sunrise Highway. It was in the town of Eastport, quite by chance, I met cousins of my former husband.

Morty's father, Theodore, set up home in the Bronx in the early 1900's when he emigrated from Lithuania. When most of Long Island was very unpopulated, one of Theodore's brother's went out East to peddle notions and other household things necessary for daily life. In this rural community he developed his business, which grew in time to become a prospering department store, the only one for miles around. I met his sons, who by this time had become prominent businessmen and one, a lawyer, was now a judge. In fact, they controlled the town, both in their real-estate holdings, and now in the political arena. When I found them and felt a warm pride for their accomplishments, I was reminded how important family roots were to me. Here I could see the store still in operation as it had been for fifty years.

My weekend wanderings once again took me to the far corners of eastern Long Island. Like in my younger years as a new suburban housewife in Levittown, I still loved the flat lands that were covered with potato plants as far as the eye could see. As I explored the destinations of Greenport, East Hampton, Sag Harbor and Montauk I discovered old burial grounds and learned to do gravestone rubbings. I was fascinated with the primitive form of art as it was developed in the new world and seen on these gravestones. I still have the rubbings of the grotesque angels and primitive icons produced by the itinerant artists of the eighteenth and early nineteenth centuries. Even traveling in Europe and South America, I have searched and studied the gravestones to understand the art and culture of the region.

Now, so energized, I decided to plan my new living room inspired by the style of Teddy Roosevelt's home, a Victorian splendor, in Cold Spring Harbor. He decorated it with the stuffed heads of animals he had collected on his hunting expeditions. On my living room wall I mounted a moose head found by a client of mine who got hooked on my strange plan. On another wall I put a print by Henri Rousseau in an ornate, antique mahogany frame. Eight small Hieronymus Bosch's prints of erotic scenes painted in the sixteenth century were in oval golden oak frames and hung along the bottom of a long window. The family room was almost as big as the living room and I had a potbelly stove installed. The Early American acquisitions I had collected on my weekend outings filled the rest of the space.

I had an insatiable drive to search for treasures and on one occasion I became excited by a big piece of, I knew not what, being held up by an auctioneer and his assistant. For some strange reason I could not resist it, and my hand shot up with my auction card waving away. I bid fifty-three dollars on this big wooden thing. Suddenly, I realized that I was the only one who wanted such an awkward, ancient artifact. Not another bid was received and I became its owner. Home I went with this big old worn out wooden piece. I pushed it around the family room and finally decided to put it in front of the couch to act as a coffee table. A friend offered to buy it for one hundred dollars the very next day. It made a big hit every time someone visited. I never saw the likes of it until some years later, on a visit to the museum at Mohonk Mountain House in New Paltz, New York. The curator assured me that I had a unique and valuable antique, a sorter used to separate wheat from the chaff. All these gems I had acquired can now be seen in the homes of my children.

I remember my Friday afternoons with my colleague Mel. It started out as two practitioners doing case supervision with one another. Slowly it became our opportunity to just relax and unwind after a long week of intense work. One week it would be lunch at an elegant restaurant in Oakdale, another time, in Northport, always overlooking water. In good weather we spent the afternoon on his sailboat. First a martini or two, and then relaxed, we would go into the wind and sail away. "Watch out for the boom" he ordered in a stern voice. What a boom was I did not know, and the first time I had to be literally pushed down to the floor of the boat. It seemed boats have a different name for everything.

One day sailing along the still waters we came across clammers digging arduously at the bottom of the bay for their catch. There I was, lazily drifting along, water all around me, and the sun and sky caressing my body, when I realized the significance of it all — wind blowing through my hair in Elmira years before, the thrill of walking through the campus at Hillside Hospital. I said to myself in my usual manner, "Lucille, you truly have arrived."

The most precious arrivals had started to come in the early 70's when my identical twin granddaughters, Tara and Robin, were delivered in 1973, courtesy of my daughter Jane. One year later Amilca arrived, a product of Tami's. My daughter Laurie and her husband Howard presented me with my grandson Daniel. And two years later Tami gave birth to her second daughter, Shannon, my last grandchild.

As the family grew so did the dinner parties. The best of all was the August pool party I gave for Grandma Sylvia, as she was now called by everyone. She was no longer thought of unpleasantly as "my stepmother." Sylvia was a small, soft-spoken, lively and wise lady who I grew to love and treasure. My father died in 1977 and just missed seeing my wonderful Sayville home. As the years went by the event grew substantially, from a small dinner on a sawbuck table beside the house, to an elaborate affair with rented round tables and chairs surrounding the large pool. Raymond and Starr along with their seven children, their assorted spouses and offspring populated these events adding warmth and laughter. I had catered platters delivered and my nephew Reed labored, making franks and top cut steaks on the grill. Pool games followed. Wine flowed and the party ended with a group playing Catch Me If You Can, with a giant inflated ball. There have been many big gatherings and formal weddings along the way but none matched the pool parties for me. I loved the interactive gayety of adults, dropping their façade and letting their "child" come out.

When my granddaughters Tara, Robin and Amilca were old enough to travel without their parents, I taught them the magic of bunburying. I never planned where we would eat or where we would stay. We were open for a new adventure. Off we went to Washington DC where my granddaughters were introduced to museums, national monuments and the importance of art. They remember the Smithsonian Institute's exhibit on the heart where we walked through the aorta to the left ventricle. Another adventure was to Philadelphia where we visited the Liberty Bell. This was in the mid 1980's when most of American cities had experienced "white flight." Philadelphia was mostly Black. We stayed in a motel in the Black community and we went to restaurants in the same area. This experience was a wake up call. My granddaughter Amilca is multiracial. Her father is African American and she identifies as Black. For the first time, I understood what it was to feel like a minority and what Amilca must feel like in our family. To this day my granddaughters remember these trips fondly and feel enriched by the experiences. I am proud that each of them inherited the spirit to travel the world.

I had only been living in my new Sayville home for three months when into my life came a tiny perky puppy. This was a gift from one of my young clients who could not think of me living alone in this big house. From that day forward puppy was always present, in my therapy room and on my new 19-foot motorboat, but only after I had a life jacket fitted for him. There I was, queen of the sea, known as one of the four women captains coming out of Oakdale, the marina a few miles from my home, and the only one with a black poodle in a white life jacket at the helm.

Child rearing is not all pleasure, as any parent will tell you. Raising a puppy can be almost as challenging. A puppy does not come with diapers, bottles, or a crib and books by Dr. Giselle or Dr. Spock, the childrearing specialists in the 50's. My puppy, who had already been named Sebastian, came in a cardboard box. First thing I did was say "No" to the name Sebastian, which did not suit this little black ball of fur, and he was stuck with the name "Puppy" for the time being.

Then I was lost. "Keep him in the bathroom, with newspaper on the floor," I was told. How to deal with his crying became another dilemma. I know I looked drained and confused, turning to friends for advice. I survived of course, with a badly soiled rug and many embarrassing moments when puppy left evidence of his presence on the floor. Finding the right food for puppy's discriminating palate was another challenge. Finally overcoming these difficulties, I was ready to have his hair trimmed. I soon learned that dogs are groomed. To find a groomer I went to the yellow pages under "groom." Not there, so I looked for animal groomer. Eventually I found a "dog groomer" who offered this service. An appointment was made and off we went, only to be presented with another decision. What kind of cut did I want, a French cut, or a...? I cannot remember all the options I had, I just remember saying that I grew up in the Jewish ghetto in the Bronx and I would just get a hair cut, no one asked me what kind I wanted. For my dog, I did not want a French cut, just a plain old cut. But the groomer could not leave well enough alone, and I was presented with a clean-cut dog, with a red bow on his head. I promptly removed the bow once we were out of sight of the very pleased hair cut man.

After he turned one year old, I officially named him "Mr. Puppy." We were a happy pair, going on our bunburying excursions when we were not on the boat. One Sunday, dressed to meet the standards of the Hampton's, we went out and this time, I left the red bow on Mr. Puppy's head and added a matching rhinestone collar. We lunched at a fine restaurant, Mr. Puppy eating his ten-dollar hamburger and fries at my feet. You guessed it, Mr. Puppy "had arrived."

This was also an important period for me as a clinician. I came to see that anxiety issues were plaguing many of my clients, preventing them from progressing in traditional talk therapy. I studied agoraphobia and the new techniques used to eliminate this problem, using behavioral therapy to overcome this debilitating condition. Here was an opportunity to integrate hypnosis into my practice.

I was especially gratified by the success I had with my client Marsha who was suffering from the fear of leaving her home, known as agoraphobia. With Marsha I was able to combine the hypnotherapy technique and my newly learned treatment, Cognitive Behavioral Therapy (CBT). In just eight sessions using hypnotherapy I was able to free her from a childhood encounter she had with her psychotic mother. While she was hypnotized, I brought her back to the night she was attacked by her mother, who jumped on top of her as she lay sleeping, attempting to strangle Marsha. With each follow up session I guided Marsha helping her visualize the experience and successfully fight off her mother and get control of the situation. In time she freed herself and with additional supportive therapy we worked on Marsha's acceptance of her mother's mental illness. Within time she came to see her mother as a very weak individual who needed care and supervision. Cured of her trauma she was able to go back to work.

Not long after we parted I received a thank you letter from her husband. They had moved to a new community where he set up a private practice as an optometrist, and Marsha went to work at a big manufacturing firm. He ended his letter on a personal note. Now that Marsha was busy working and decorating their new home, she was freed from her overactive libido that had been an added stress on their relationship.

Mr. Puppy often enriched my therapeutic experiences. As I would bring a client out of the trance, Puppy would begin stretching and slowly move his head from side to side as if he too had been in a calming hypnotic state. I also felt calm and pleased, rewarded by a great sense of accomplishment.

I wasn't your typical "armchair" therapist. In fact, while I was working with women from the Islip Women's Center on assertiveness training, I concocted an unconventional plan, both daring and dangerous. Alice, one of the women who belonged to the center, wanted to separate from her rich, abusive husband, but could not break away because of his threats on her life. She did not want his money, she simply wanted her freedom. On one occasion when I tried to help her, Alice's husband physically threatened me for interfering in a personal family matter. There were a few incidents when Alice called the police for help. They would come to her house, but were instructed from above to quiet the conflict. The police did not see their job as saving a woman in a dangerous domestic situation. I met with Alice and her support group and presented my plan for her escape. These timid women, who themselves where struggling for greater autonomy, were now being asked to go to Alice's house on a designated day. They would have to move all of Alice's and her children's belongings and put them in the waiting truck. I was to play interference, dressed in a tailored suit befitting a social worker, should any one appear to halt our work. Once the task was done at the house, the group was to reassemble at the new modest rented apartment in Patchoque. They readily agreed to help in carrying out the plan. On the scheduled day we all appeared, a bit nervous but ready for action. They all worked in silence together, carrying chairs, tables, beds, you name it, big or small, they worked hard and fast and with great energy completed the task.

We all kept the secret. I was not reported to the authorities as having inappropriately used my CSW credentials in a domestic conflict. Alice and her children were now going to be supported by her retired father on his limited Social Security check. From that day on I was known as the Liberation Therapist of Suffolk County and I was flattered when a few local bookstore owners asked me for lists of recommended self-help readings for women. *Our Bodies Our Selves*, *Assertiveness Training* and *I'm OK, You're OK* were just some of the books I suggested. Even the manager of my bank asked if I would meet with the newly emerging employee's women's group to answer many of their concerns.

A new area of work for me was with young men who were suffering from symptoms of Post-Traumatic Stress Disorder as a result of their Vietnam War experiences. This was complicated work, which left me with deep sadness for the victims of this senseless war. Though Vietnam veterans had their own counselors in their veteran organizations, I worked with them on problems with their marriages, relationships and employment. This helped me comprehend how my ex-husband Morty's war experience injured him for many years because, in fact, he too suffered from this disorder.

Connections from my professional life enriched me socially. I met Sue, who was to become a life-long friend, at a Social Work conference. At one of the workshops we learned we were neighbors and I immediately invited her to join me on a canoe outing. We both relished being physically challenged and made plans for our first trip the following Sunday. Sue enjoyed it so much that she asked if her husband Norman could come along the next time. Always looking for another person to join in the excitement of this newfound passion of mine, I welcomed him. We picked up Norman in Bayport at the Unitarian Fellowship, a religious and socially minded group of people from many different faiths and ethnicities. This was at a time in my life when I began to recognize the need for a spiritual home. With all my wandering, my different jobs, and my exciting and adventurous life, there was still a place inside me that felt empty. Norman invited me to meet his friends over coffee at the Unitarian's beautiful colonial building on the Long Island Sound. This was a group of truly open-minded and free-spirited people who took me in. I was hooked, not only on canoeing but now, on the Unitarian Fellowship. Although I am an atheist I am spiritual at my core and always drawn to community.

After a few years of emotional, financial and professional stability suddenly my bubble burst. My fun loving and creative son-in-law was diagnosed with colon cancer in an advanced stage and was not expected to live beyond six months. This was a devastating blow. Howard was more like a nurturing father to me, the one I never had, and now I was to face another world shattering loss.

First my mother when I was eight, then Freddy, my seventeen year old nephew and now Howard, only forty. I remember putting the phone receiver down, having just learned the diagnosis from my daughter Laurie. Numb and in shock, I slowly said to my friend Ellen, "Howard is going to die. I think I'll miss most of all the joy I feel in my heart with Howard in my life." Though I went on living, even taking a tour of China and participating in wonderful windjammer trips off the coast of Maine, there remained a deep sadness within me.

Howard fought hard to ensure that every minute of his remaining days were meaningful, spending time with his young son Daniel, and continuing his beloved hobby of painting. Howard produced a massive amount of artwork, and he was talented, going beyond the realistic to portray his inner fantasy world. During his final days, his paintings began to depict his diminishing life. In one, he is seen settled deep into an easy chair with angels floating around him. The angels are dressed in nurse's uniforms and I could sense his comfort with these caretakers easing him into the next world.

Breaking all odds, Howard lived for a little more than two years. We spent weekends together when we could and on occasion listened to Bernie Siegel's meditation tapes. In the late 70's and early 80's Dr. Siegel introduced the then revolutionary idea of the mind-body connection to the alternative medical community. His book *Love, Medicine and Miracles: Lessons Learned about Self-Healing from a Surgeon's Experience with Exceptional Patients* has become a classic, and his audio cassette *Meditations for Enhancing Your Immune System* gave solace to both Howard and me. Other simple things gave Howard comfort, like my preparing him a meal. It was a pleasure to watch his friends rub his arms and feet, bringing warmth into his withering body. Our last day together was spent at the Metropolitan Museum of Art viewing the wooden carvings brought to this country from Africa. After a wonderful lunch in the posh dining room we returned home, tired but exhilarated. He died a few weeks later, fighting to his last breath for the life he so loved. His final request to me, in his own words, was "give my son culture."

I have done a great deal of reflecting about why this relationship was so special and why Howard's death affected me so profoundly. I had known romance when I was a sixteen year old adolescent in love and had known passion as a forty year old in a tumultuous affair. I had inspirational friendships with comrades from my progressive political life, and supportive colleagues from my professional life. But Howard was different.   He filled a void that I have come to understand as unconditional acceptance and love for me — something I had never received from my family.

In 1986, three years after Howard died, I was hit with a strange disease, new on the scene, with no known cure. I have learned since then that stress, for some people, is so great that in time it breaks down immune functions of the body. I developed recurring pain in the upper right side of my back, and with it there were chills, then bouts of bronchitis and shingles. The greatest change, and most disturbing, was my loss of energy. I felt exhausted all the time and I had the sense that I was walking in a brain fog. I could not shake this incessant malaise and became frightened and worried about what this would mean to my practice.

I had never paid much attention to my body and here I was at sixty-five facing such a devastating illness without a name. People of my generation thought little about health, let alone the aging process. When it came to cancer, it was whispered as the "Big C." Preventative medicine and new medical technology was completely out-of-our landscape before the 1980's.

But what about our bodies? There was shame for my growing feminine figure when I was thirteen. There were admonitions from my aunts to stand straight. At forty, after experiencing great back pain, I learned that I had scoliosis and would possibly end up seriously disabled. It was at this point in my life that I was introduced to chiropractic care that helped keep my spine in alignment and saved me from becoming disabled. I learned about lumps in the breast when one was found in mine. It was removed and everyone was relieved to learn that it was benign. Then came the pills for high blood pressure. After complaining about pains in my fingers my stepmother Sylvia reassured me, it was only arthritis. Then came the burning sensation in a toe. Again, Sylvia to the rescue, "It was arthritis." The sudden electric shock that shot through my body, and again, "It's only arthritis." It came in many forms and I began to tolerate these strange intrusions repeating to myself Sylvia's accepting mantra "It's only arthritis!" We were complacent and thought it was indulgent to even admit to health concerns. I hardly paid any attention to this body of mine. Although I began to hear of other people's serious health issues it had little to do with me and I went on with my busy life focusing on my children, school, work, and romance. My life was hectic, rushed, and like most people's, full of stress.

During the period of my full-time private practice in Sayville, a doctor warned me that I could no longer put so much weight on my vulnerable spine. I purchased two recliners — one for my treatment room and one for the group therapy room. I was also warned that sitting for long periods of time would be hard on my circulatory system. My response was to join a gym immediately. On and on it went, learning about different parts of my body as one or another broke down. Now, in 1986, I was faced with severe fatigue.

The doctor I sought out to help me with this debilitating condition asked me if I was sad or despondent, for it seemed to him I had symptoms of depression. My response was that I had a serious depression after Howard died but I did not have chills, a fever, a sore throat and shooting pains throughout my entire body.

It took two more years and visits to many doctors before finally Dr. Brus, a specialist in this new disease, declared that indeed, I did have one of the new viruses encompassed under the diagnosis of Chronic Fatigue Immune Dysfunction also know as Chronic Fatigue Syndrome (CFS).

My whole body, all 165 pounds of me, felt drained, just wanting to sleep and let the world pass me by. My illness made it impossible to go on working and I had to give up my practice. I laughingly told friends, I would even have to give up my men — my yardman, my handy man, my boatman, and even my garbage man.

And with the same adventurous spirit I always had, I went for it. Yes, on to becoming a retired Floridian.

5

My Retirement

So on to Florida where I joined the legions of retirees. My sister Vivian had settled in Florida years before and encouraged me to live close to her so she could help care for me through the difficult and frequent bleak days of this illness. Though I felt raw and found the move difficult, there was a hidden surprise. I was reacquainted with my nephew Teddy after many years of little contact. Following the death of his brother Freddy, over thirty years ago, my close extended family was just never the same, which created a distance between all of us.

Teddy had become a science high school teacher and was living in Hollywood, Florida. Now he emerged into my life with open arms and supported me emotionally through all the years of my illness. With my sister Vivian and my nephew Teddy, this "old" family, became my "new" family. Teddy and I spent many afternoons walking on the beach talking about philosophical ideas and planning new adventures while Vivian was busy in her garage studio chipping away at large stones creating brilliant works of art. When I needed help to move a piece of old furniture found at a thrift store, Teddy was there to carry it to my living room and along with many of Vivian's sculptures, my condo began to resemble a museum. For the first time in many years, the memories of my Levittown family felt comfortable. This family was now back in my life.

I had more to learn about the multi-layered ramifications of CFS. This illness had already directly impacted my livelihood, people's perceptions of me and the medical community's ability to deliver appropriate care. On top of this, as a Medicare patient, I began to understand the medical industry through a different eye. I found articles about doctors in Florida being charged with fraud for administering unnecessary tests and procedures and billing Medicare. Although I did not have a heart condition, I had undergone multiple tests for my heart, running up bills of many thousands of dollars at a great cost, not only to Medicare, but also to my emotional stability. And how the doctors in Florida loved my body. They found so much wrong with me that I did not have time to learn the names of all these failing parts. My entire body seemed on the verge of collapse and I turned all of me over to their tests and procedures. I was frightened for my life.

Sadly, in the 1980's, the medical community was so confounded by the enigmatic Chronic Fatigue Syndrome, it was easier for many physicians to diagnose people as suffering from depression. In fact, it was even considered by some doctors as a modern day form of female "Hysteria" because 80% of the diagnosed cases were women. The controversy over CFS as a physiological or psychological condition has raged until only recently. Now it is more commonly understood to have a physiological basis. After twenty years of the first known cases, of which I was one, there still is no treatment and little to no money for research. And yet, in the United States the incidence of CFS is even higher than HIV/AIDS.

I slowly became revitalized and in touch with my innate energy and my need to become proactive. I joined the newly formed Chronic Fatigue Syndrome National Organization and went to every conference held in the area.

I had learned over the years to reach out to others

for support and comfort, first the Fogelson family of my youth then the Young Communist League and my wonderful Consciousness Raising Group in Far Rockaway. As someone who came from a fragmented and unsupportive family, I had learned at a young age to reach out to others much like myself. Now I joined a support group for those suffering from CFS and could feel as one with others as we moaned and lamented our fate.

Having gained more strength I threw myself into the thick of things and joined the National Organization of Women in Florida and led a Saturday book club. We were examining books with a focus on the author's treatment of women. Weren't the participants dismayed when I found one of Danielle Steel's books commendable for her positive portrayal of her heroine, and ripped apart the work of the feminist writer, Marilyn French for her negative comments on Cuba?

I went to every demonstration NOW organized in the state from Tallahassee to the mall in Boca Raton. In the course of all this activity I rediscovered Dorothy, a long lost friend from my Levittown days. Dorothy and I became activist buddies. We took a long bus trip to Cape Canaveral protesting the building up of the United States war machine, both of us in red caps, posters in hand, chanting anti-war slogans and chomping on our sandwiches and drinking sodas. I remember hugging Dorothy as we looked into each other's eyes and, without a word, saluted the long years we had spent together, going back to our Levittown days, always fighting the "good fight."

Dorothy, now frail and bent, is still at it. She writes a column for the local newspaper and donates money (a dollar in each envelope) to hundreds of progressive organizations around the country. And here I am on my computer hooked up to the Internet, where I join others fighting for better health care for the elderly and against the "evil doer", George Bush.

Though I was still sick with CFS I had free time to immerse myself in additional community involvement. It was at this time that I came to know an energetic young woman named Pam who was an activist in NOW. Together we accepted an assignment to represent NOW on the annual Martin Luther King committee. This committee was assigned to organize a yearly parade to be held in downtown Delray Beach, an impoverished Black community. Pam and I were the only two white women on the committee. This experience brought back memories of my time in Mississippi when racial polarization was the norm. Just imagine my joy in walking in the Martin Luther

King parade through downtown Delray, where the impact of Jim Crow had lasted years after the Civil Rights Movement.

Over time I came to realize that many Black churches were in fact as conservative as some of the mainstream religious institutions. The local Black churches controlled this committee and chose the speakers for all the events we were organizing. These conservative Black leaders would never challenge the political establishment. They rejected all "outsiders" including the NAACP (National Association for the Advancement of Colored People). In spite of this, Pam and I tried to push the committee and we recommended that they reach out to the newly growing Haitian community and involve them in the parade. This was rejected. I continued to participate in many other functions in the Black community, making friends, but the residue of racism affected our social relationships. The friendships never flourished. We were simply set apart from each other in our own ghettos. I felt badly but came to accept these conditions and continued to participate.

Although I surrounded myself with my new friends and organizations in Florida, there was a persistent aching pain about the distance I had with my children.

Over the years my relationships with my three daughters had become strained. I thought that going to Florida would relieve me of this sense of rejection. Although the change of location was helpful, I came to understand that one must deal with unfinished business from the past before moving on.

My anger and frustration erupted one day when Laurie phoned me and told me that she was not going to move to Riverdale to an apartment in a private home, as planned, where her son Daniel would be able to play outdoors and attend one of the best public schools in New York City. She had decided to remain in her apartment in Manhattan. This meant Daniel would have to go to private school and survive in what I believed was then a dangerous city. I ranted and raged, hung up the phone, called my sister Vivian, told her what had just happened, then proceeded to weep and wail. In a short time Vivian and Teddy arrived but I would not respond to their pleading for me to open the door. They kept banging and I finally relented and let them in. With determination and conviction, Vivian and Teddy took me to my first Al Anon meeting.

Twelve-step programs like AA and Al Anon are usually reserved for the addicted and the family of the substance abusers. However, the programs can be helpful for anyone struggling with issues of dependency and co-dependency, as I was. In the twelve-step program, I learned to detach from the pain of the past. Al Anon, in its fourth step, requires you to focus on yourself and your shortcomings and wisely directs the members to take responsibility for themselves eschewing the seductive role of being a victim. I learned what I had done to cause my children's detachment. After accepting my part in these failed relationships, I was able to progress through each step and "let my higher power grant me the serenity to accept the things I cannot change, and the courage to change the things I can, and the wisdom to know the difference." The twelve-step program is an on-going and internal process requiring personal motivation to revisit each step throughout a member's life.

Looking back I am gratified and surprised at my ability to reach out to others and gain support from the groups I joined and the causes I embraced. An important concept I learned in Al Anon was "acceptance." I use the twelve-step approach to many things in my life. It has helped me accept the aging process and its impact on my body. I now live with an osteoarthritic spine and macular degeneration, causing the sudden loss of vision in my left eye, and the declining vision in my right eye. Al Anon has also helped me see my uniqueness and my strengths.

Obviously I have been a collector all my life — antiques, hobbies, family photos, old furnishings, vintage jewelry and even interesting men. I have also collected friends. Pam, her husband and their little two-year-old daughter Caroline became my extended family in Florida. Their home came to be my home, and I embraced the warmth, love and mental stimulation I found there. By now I had collected Sue and Marie in Sayville and in the near future it would be Katherine, who I would eventually meet in Woodstock, New York. These women, all in there forties, have fortified me and today we are still there for each other. The impact of the Women's Liberation Movement has created this profound consciousness that has become so deeply integrated into our psyche.

Here I was in 1990 living in my condo in Kingspoint, one of the communities on the east coast of Florida catering to working-class Jewish retirees. While I was at a party I heard condescending comments about the people from Kingspoint being "pushy" and "uncultured." The host quickly came to my defense and said, "She is not like them!" Then I said to the man sitting next to me with a can of beer in his hand, "When I first came in I thought you were a redneck. You see, we all stereotype one another!" The room went silent. Even at a NOW meeting, where I hardly expected this, I heard a disparaging statement from one of the members that the people from Kingspoint are "aggressive, pushy Jews." In the future, I avoided telling people that, in fact, I came from Kingspoint. Again, I learned that I was living in one of the worst places to come from. I had reached the bottom in the eyes of many around me.

In 1993 I decided I wanted to be closer to my family in the Northeast so I purchased a summer home in Woodstock, New York dividing my time between Florida and New York. I introduced myself to the new crowd as an artist who wintered in Florida, now living in a small retreat outside Woodstock in the town of West Hurley. Again, my aunts were not alone in their prejudices. It was everywhere, even in Woodstock, the land of the so-called "liberated." So, I never let on that my summerhouse was a mobile home in a trailer park.

However, I cannot imagine a better place to come from. Here, in Woodstock, in this artistic and progressive community, I could dress in the bright

151

blues and purples I so favor and accessorize with the ethnic beaded necklaces I brought back from my travels. And I would never leave my home without wearing earrings dangling down to my shoulders.

At the Unitarian Congregation, I would dress in anything my mood suggested at the time. My home group in the twelve-step program was held at Christ Church in the center of town and our Saturday meetings always ended with some of us eating at Marie's, a favorite local restaurant. There we could eat a sandwich and have a cup of coffee for two dollars. I got to know everyone in town, sharing the local gossip and social concerns about the community and some of the people who lived there. At Marie's I could sit for hours on end and chat with the local Judge who made Marie's his home away from home. Everyone in town knew where the Judge could be found and from time to time, one of the waitresses would call him to the phone, and there, behind the counter, he would counsel people on personal and town matters.

One of my greatest treats was to hear Alf Evers, the local historian, well into his nineties, talk about the beginnings and development of Woodstock. In his book *Woodstock: History of an America Town* Evers describes how Woodstock was established as a haven for free thinkers who pursued their vision of a Utopian, self-sufficient community. This community is constantly redefining itself as successive generations of bohemians, much like myself, and city exiles settle here.

I had found roots in the Woodstock community by making a commitment to the Unitarian Congregation and the twelve-step program. With my connection to Al Anon and the Unitarians I can go anywhere around the world, wherever there is a twelve-step group and a Unitarian Fellowship, and feel welcomed. I have finally found not one but two spiritual homes.

Advancing my artwork, hiking, bunburying and soaking in the music at the historic Maverick Concert Barn, my life in Woodstock was the richest and most well rounded I had ever had. Suddenly, out of the blue, I was brought down by another major insult to my body unrelated to CFS. The severe and almost paralyzing pain in my spine drove me to the emergency room time and time again. After several hospitalizations, I had a procedure to relieve the pain — an injection of a nerve-blocking drug. I thank Dr. Gamberg every day for his care and the successful outcome that has eliminated the disabling pain.

With the confluence of continued weakness, extreme weight loss, my fragile spine and the progressive loss of my vision, I had to design a new

153

plan for my future. Unfortunately, my daily activities, including taking care of my home and garden were compromised. I could no longer drive and needed public transportation, which was not available in the Woodstock area. Though romantic in concept, living in the woods, outside of town, turned out not to be so good for someone of my age. I decided to move where I would have access to good public transportation and closer to my family. I found a studio apartment in The Kittay House, an assisted living facility which is part of The Jewish Home and Hospital in the Bronx.

All three of my daughters and three of my grandchildren live in New York City and, through all the bumps and hurdles, we have grown into a very loving and special family. Jane has a thriving private practice as a clinical social worker, specializing in child and family treatment. Laurie is a holistic nurse who practices healing bodywork and teaches her techniques as well. And Tami's powerful social issue documentaries have appeared at film festivals, on public television, HBO and throughout the world. My daughters have country homes filled with many of my old treasures acquired throughout my life's travels and what's most important, they continue to enjoy our tradition of bunburying with their partners, their children, and now their grandchildren.

Now back to the beginning of my story. Remember, it started with me strolling down Kingsbridge Road in the Bronx, smiling and taking in the sounds and smells of the city. Here I am at 85 years old, back in the Bronx, the place I left at twenty-two. A place I promised I would never return to.

I think to myself, it has been a long journey and I have learned a great deal. Now, living with seniors, as we old people are called, I see a problem with the American obsession with individualism and independence. Much of this philosophy comes from the writer Horatio Alger whose "rags-to-riches" story became famous in the mid 1800's. His writings promote the myth that poor and disadvantaged people could overcome tremendous obstacles on their own and build the American Dream against all odds.

The fact is no one does it on his or her own. I climbed the ladder, but there was always someone there, either pushing or pulling me. The myth of "independence", that we act alone, has a direct and sometimes negative impact on all of us, especially the elderly. I see many giving in to their infirmities and passively opting for complete dependency, or fighting, resisting help, and refusing to surrender some of their independence. I share with all who will listen, "I am independent when I can be, and dependent when I need to be." That is my mantra. I am at peace with myself. I admit, sometimes I am able to accomplish the task of crossing the street independently, but I accept the help of a big strong man standing next to me, happily leaning heavily on his arm.

Today I live in the Kittay House in the Kingsbridge area of the Bronx among "uncommon" people who love to tell me stories about the places they come from: Puerto Rico, Russia, Hungary, Ghana, and Vietnam, to name a few, and about their new lives in America. I feel at home among friendly people who not only enjoy telling me tales from their countries of birth but who are curious about where I have come from.

Here on Kingsbridge Road, people from all parts of Central and Latin America help me cross streets, assist me as I attempt to board buses, hold my hand, or squeeze my arm lovingly as they call me "mama!" I feel their warmth surging through my body and I know that I am loved and accepted, a member of the community. I have become a member of the Unitarian Fellowship Congregation in Manhattan and, sorry to say, here in the Bronx, though welcomed at Al Anon meetings, I still do not understand Spanish, the language of this community.

Feeling comfortable in my wrinkled skin with

nothing to hide, I now have no class, no pretensions, no more climbing and no more struggles between conformity and non-conformity. I am just strolling along doing my thing and proudly telling all who care to listen, "I live at the Jewish Home and Hospital and I am growing old in the Bronx."

Afterthoughts

Writing the story of my life has been very illuminating. I was surprised to note my ability to be as adventurous as I was. Sometimes fearful and extremely anxious, I plowed ahead, taking chances, time and again.

It suggests something important to me. In my years in the psychological field, we believed that environment was the cause of all mental aberrations, and "poor mother", she took quite a rap for anything that went wrong in the development of the child. Now we have come of age, and gene theory has taken over. The scientists have gone to the other extreme, only gene theory matters. We know now that my learning disability was inherited. There was that little old gene, lurking somewhere, coming out in one or another of us. My father passed it on to me, to my brother Raymond, and my sister Vivian, and in turn, I passed it to my daughter Tami. I always blessed the fact that, because we were not able to spell and our reading skills were limited, there was no way we could become secretaries. Tami became an educator and documentary filmmaker. Raymond is the Founder and CEO of a major plumbing corporation and, at the age of ninety, my sister Vivian is a very accomplished abstract expressionist sculptor. I blossomed as a social worker where my organization and analytic skills could flourish.

When I visited Israel many years ago, I had the chance to meet my cousin Abraham for the first time. He could not speak English although everyone in his family and community were bilingual. When his wife whispered to me that he could never learn English no matter how hard he tried, I jumped from my chair and kissed him and said, "You truly are my cousin." He had the very same affliction we have, that troublesome gene. I looked beyond the unwanted gene and now I wonder, perhaps my adventurous personality and sense of humor is somehow connected to a "daredevil" gene. This gene, if indeed it is a gene, I detect in my siblings as well. I hope someday it can be isolated and implanted into everyone.

Now at eighty plus I realize that aging itself creates the greatest challenge for each of us as human beings. There is the loss of physical abilities, mental acuity, and loved ones. As a result of these losses, there is an even greater need for psychological adaptability and strength. I remain passionate, and courageous enough to write this memoir. I leave you with three attributes that have helped me come to terms with personal challenges, old age and death — *passion, courage and flexiblity.*

Again I repeat, it was a hard life, but I continue to *"dream the impossible dream."*

Life goes on and I have to accept the fact that struggles and growth will continue. And so it is, I now have to deal with a new language, or better put, the use of my new ABC's.

Not a simple undertaking. This knowledge is critical to my survival. There is the support of the AARP, EPIC and SCRIE. I have yet to deal with the IRT and the BMT. To fill out my day there is the YWHA for my exercise program. The JCC provides me with taxi service to my MD and waiting for me at home is JASA. They supply me with a social worker to explain the workings of my new ABC's.

As I have said before, I am sure more surprises are still to come. I just hope I am not too old to meet the new challenges.

Oops — I almost forgot

Norvac   take 1x daily
Aveca   take before bedtime
Celexa   take 1x daily

Luiten	take before lunch
Bilberry	take 1x daily
Vitamin B,C,E	take together

Must run now. I'm off to look for a DVD player and an iPod. "They" say it is something I must have.

Books:

Narciss and Goldmund by Herman Hesse

Maybe, Maybe Not by Robert Fulghum

All I Ever Needed to Know I Learned in Kindergarten by Robert Fulghum

Codependent No More by Melody Beattie

The Importance of Being Earnest by Oscar Wilde

Songs:

Imagine by John Lennon

To Dream the Impossible Dream Music by Mitch Leigh and Lyrics by Joe Darion

These are segments from the letters I wrote to my daughter Tami while she was traveling and studying in Mexico, Cuba and Latin America.

July 25, 1967
Dear Tami,

Hope you got back okay! Hot in town! Al just raved about how well you look! I'm so pleased hearing it from someone else! It sure was my impression too! ...Now, a few driving lessons and I'll never see the car again. You sure are going to be a good driver... do they have Jeeps on the farms of Cuba?

Busy week! Concert in the park tonight with George... Starr and Raymond's tomorrow (finally will see their house)... the staff going to Central Park Thursday night for biking, eating and rowing...

The Negro situation gets hotter! eh! Glad we saw firsthand.

I'll call Saturday.
Love,
Mother

[Upon learning about the Newark Riots, Tami and I drove to Newark to see what was actually happening. The riot was in response to a police officer killing an unarmed black man. We witnessed the National Guard unloading truck filled with watermelons onto the streets.]

164

Dear Tami

Ellen and I will be having dinner together this week and then we will be going to a meeting where Rap Brown is scheduled to speak. Of course, now that he is in jail I don't know what will happen. Maybe they will raise the $25,000 or perhaps turn the meeting into a mass demonstration… Hurry home, they need you. Someone called today from Viet Nam Summer to ask for your help – he said they need you in the fall and then some – until the war is over.

Love,
Mother

Dear Tami

I never realized the joy that a photo could be! There you are before me all the time when I suffer the indignities that are mine at my job at Cancer Care. So please send me your pictures as frequently as you can… I do not wish to take the edge off this request by telling you that I now know the power that the "machine" has over us. The establishment can grind you down to a 9 to 5 er – quick lunch at 12 and down to Orbachs and the end of the day arrives, your lungs clogged – air gone out of your body and the only thought left to drag your weary – deflated – empty body home. The shock of this came to me last night when I sat down to write to you. "How void my day had been." But, on to the tomorrows – of learning and again working fruitfully. In the mean time I am further freeing myself of my suburban middle-class past!

On the newsy side!

Laurie, Sue, Ruth and I are registered for yoga… I'm going to see Richie Havens — a real fan of his — but I shall miss your presence… Our singles group – I've taken over the leadership and we are going to make it meaningful – discussions, etc...

The election looks dry and boring! No one here is at all excited. Humphrey knows he faces an uphill fight – He unfortunately can't even mount a molehill.

Good night sweet one

Till tomorrow
Me

Dear Tami

How great a thrill – to get your letter! Though you did not mention it I'm sure you have received mine. This is <u>no. 4</u>. Just returned from a weekend at Fire Island! How reminiscent of the time I visited you there. I went to the house you were at! Found 2 that could have been it, The Viking on Ocean Rd. and The Balcony on the next road. <u>Which one?</u> The place we swam at? I even ate dinner at the restaurant we went to. I spent the entire time alone, basking in the sun, meditating, walking and enjoying my aloneness and finally, finally I caught up with all my feelings. And of course they were mainly of you... How strange it should be that of all the people in the world, you who I love most, should be so far away. Thoughts come to me – like remember when you said, "Let's go to Africa." <u>Well you have begun the adventure.</u> I am so very glad. Or the time we went to Nantucket...lobster, my shopping, you cooking... All these little things over the last few years. What I have liked best has been the quiet between us... the silences have been rich with sympathy and understanding... And I had time to savor the memories of days and evenings spent with Sophie. How warm they make me feel. And the day with the minister in his church on the hill – dancing at

Peg-Leg Bates– East Village Inn. But special of all is the meals prepared at our home on Mountain Rd. (Union City) with you.

I have struggled against this pain I feel at not having you at my side. I get angry with myself for it – why must Lucille Gold suffer so. But that is Lucille Gold – for all that, she has great joys too, the joy of knowing that some day in the future we will be together again, and both more mature and richer for the experiences. One must learn to love richly and give all with the full knowledge that it must lead to many painful eventualities…

It troubles me that you speak of the "sex starved middle-class fuckers." To hate fully is good too! But why all this hatred for young beings who are not fully mature – who are human beasts with animal needs – not yet mature enough or in control of themselves. I don't know any of them but your anger speaks of feelings that go beyond them. I worry about what is behind your hatred… Must it wait to be explored? Will this unresolved problem prevent you from enjoying some of the joys that are possible in a relationship with a man? <u>Let us speak more on this.</u>

No more – I'm falling asleep.

Love,

Mother

Wed 10/9/68

Dear Tami –

Enclosed article on Mexico – more will follow. There have been no demonstrations here in this country to support the jailed and killed Mexican students, but then, maybe I'm not getting reports.

Love and kisses
Mother

Oct 18, 1968

Dear Comrade,

Two letters from you one day after another and I'm ecstatic. Strange but the only one who spells worse than I do is you so why should I ask you if I spelled ecstatic right?

Today I was awakened by the phone at 9AM and it was Ron returned from a period away. Though I was still very sleepy I did hear him say that he has left CORE. Plans to go into business with some of the leaders who were disaffected and may even go back to school. I was not all with it so promised to call him back and arrange to see him.

"Forever" What significance does the word have for you? … I just spent one minute contemplating the word and all I could think of was… life, and things of one's life weave in and out, recurring over and over again in different patterns, the only thing that doesn't come back is Freddy… therefore the only finality is death… Within life there is every hope – every possibility. How wonderful! I shall attempt not to die for a long time. Especially since I have found a new contentment. And I also look forward to a future with you again by my side. Maybe grandchildren. Certainly a few more dinner parties prepared by us jointly — do come home with a few recipes. I'm so tired of making turkey for our guests. I'm going away for Thanksgiving weekend because I don't think I can face it this year without you.

Short takes:

Job interviews – one as Director of Recreation in Montefiore Hosp…. Another one at Morningside Hosp in Glen Ridge…wouldn't it be funny if I went to work a half a block from where we lived in Glen Ridge…

Where is Laurie, you ask? At home with me. We only use Jane's apt when we remain in New York City for the evening. We are getting on very well together, drawing closer in our need to compensate for your absence. She is growing stronger and though her therapy has not been of long duration it has been very beneficial…

…I saw Fran last week on a picket line in front of the Americana – anti-Humphrey picket. The cops were wicked, rode right into the crowd and made many arrests. Fran received your letter and promises to write. Tami, people get so caught up in life and don't realize how others count on them – so don't be too harsh if your dear ones don't seem to respond as you would have them do. I remember that I wouldn't write to my father for <u>months</u> on end. I would just reappear 6 months later. He never reprimanded me!... Talking of Pop… he looks great. I was up to dinner last night. Laurie's friend Lenny is home for a funeral, his friend killed in the Vietnam War. Tonight I feel I can go on and on. But I'll save some of the tidbits for tomorrow.

Love,
LG

Tuesday 1PM
Oct 22, 1968
Dearest Tami –

In my last letter I wrote about it being an international week. Oh dear – how international I was to learn Sunday night I came down with the Hong Kong Flu and here I sit in the den with the sun baking on me and trying to enjoy the enforced rest. Chills run up and down my spine and I keep sniffling but nonetheless I am content with plans to read all afternoon. This is in preparation for what I want to discuss with you in this letter. <u>Tactics!</u>

3PM
Well, I have finished both articles and reflected a bit. My first thought is that everyone talks about the SDS and other student forces as if they were the sum total of the opposition in our country. There are other forces – the Negroes, and socialist parties, and the left middle-class forces. To talk of strategy and tactics of the youth and students is to see within what societal sphere they operate. Only then can you see what <u>tactics they have available</u>. Economic arena? No. Political arena? No. What constituents do they control? No institution but

the university and the street.

<u>Thought 2</u> – on alternatives to anti-activity. For once a movement of the people (not limited to the way off Left) is saying our society stinks – to hell with pretense and sham. On moral grounds, on humanistic grounds we fail. There must be something better. I almost think it wrong if the left movement at this point would put forth a program or solution. (Alternatives at this point would be precipitous because the people are not yet at a revolutionary point.) That is long in coming.

Thought 3

Sure there is much to criticize in the left movement. But not what is being developed among the youth. (A terrible failure of the left is not to see that tactics must be developed at different levels all meshing with the overall strategic objective.)

<u>Long term objective</u> – socialist reform

<u>Short term</u> –	end war in Viet Nam
	freedom for the Negro
	democratic reform

| <u>Strategy</u> – | harassment of the power elite |

realign forces of the people

<u>Tactics</u> – 1. confrontation and disruption
2. exposure of hypocrisy of democracy
4. political activity within existing parties
5. activity in unions relating working men's interests to moral issues

So let's not berate the great job being done by the new left. Most important is to get some old left into the work not being done.

More another day – I'm tired now! Sure would appreciate your thoughts on the subject.

Love,
Mother

Friday AM
Dear Tami –

Just a short note because I am emotionally spent! No special cause – just don't feel like thinking today. Yesterday I rode out to Bamberger's in Wayne. I like the unhurried atmosphere of the place. Had lunch – ambled around and just when I was beginning to feel sorry I had ever come out I found a nice Borganza coat – nice and bright champagne, double-breasted and better put together than you would expect at $26. Now as if that weren't treat enough I chanced to be approached by a woman who wanted my opinion of her selection of a dark, drab, grey coat trimmed with dismal, dull maroon. Poor dear, she didn't have a chance with me, and before the exchange was over she had in her possession a bright champagne double-breasted $26 Borganza coat. How complete my day!

The evening was quiet – Laurie and John studying for her test on Monday and mother sewing a hem. We then went to Lola's to watch the 11PM news – George Wallace being harassed at Madison Sq. Garden – the teacher's strike – the war in Viet Nam. Then to hear Julio rant and rage about the minority groups. Al said he thinks the world's going mad and Laurie sat there smugly and said she thought a nice revolution was in order... Life of a mother recovering from the ravages of the flu...

Tonight – hair set and all pretty, I will have dinner with Hy and Edith, then to a movie about the Bay of Pigs and something on Viet Nam. (I want to review it for a possible showing by my group Singles on the Left.)

Tomorrow out with Nina for a matinee – then the Singles of the Left Party.

Jane has flu – happy with Paul

Love,
Mother

Sunday AM –
Coffee – the NY Times –
a clean house –
the sun streaming in on me in the den –
quiet and <u>you</u>.

Dear Tami,

I am content! But it was only yesterday that I cried as I reached for a cake mix only to remember that you would not be there in the kitchen to make it up. Alas, I will get used to it! I am so very pleased with your getting the opportunity to witness first hand the many varieties of life. I fear for your safety in the troubles existing in Mexico – yet know that one must engage in a meaningful life – one of struggle – one of daring. I know full well that the fascist trend that we see today is in response to the great surge forward of the people – let us not look at in despair or dismay – rather, see it as a challenge.

Our shortcoming is that we are not prepared ideologically or organizationally to deal with the threat. There is great division still among our forces and this may be our downfall. But even here I do not become disheartened because it is my strong belief that history does not move evenly – it is often the case that <u>historical necessity</u> propels, and out of this necessity comes the possibility of greater clarity and unity. (Of course this is only a possibility – an examination of the black movement – the labor movement and the leftist movement does not portend great hope.) Could it be the youth, the students, who give us the lead? I have said in the recent months that it will be around <u>issues</u> that unity and action will take place. I have seen that happen in historical periods such as the '30's around the issue of hunger and poverty. It was around the demands to end the war in Russia that the revolution was born. But in every case it was only with a capable Left Party that success was achieved. The period ahead will be interesting! Nixon as president! Inflation and the possibility of a recession! Interesting times. I do hope that you are well mobilized and working hard to grow in all areas. I spoke to you once about art – of seeing technique as a tool – so too is knowledge – a tool. I hope in this period you will be developing yourself to sharpen your ability to use the tools for constructive betterment of society.

Nina spoke about an impatience in you which I have seen. "Impatience" is a great thing because without it the youth of today would not have thrown off the hold of parental values! All power to "impatience". It is only when this attitude leads to general negative and hopeless resolution that it becomes destructive. So go on being impatient – don't accept the status quo! The one caution is that you not be led in your dissent from positive action to change what you don't like…

Sandy went with me to hear Richie Havens at Philharmonic Hall Friday night! Can you believe it! After such a short time – a year and a half – to sell out the house. My first reaction was one of disappointment. He wasn't stoned – he was so straight and his singing just didn't have that soul I love him for. But he has moved to a new plateau of musicianship and he is on the way to developing something new instrumentally, new sounds, new dimensions! He hasn't gotten there yet but I think he is well on his way – time will tell where this will take him. An interesting development and I am glad to be a witness to his movement. (But I must find a new soul brother who moves me in that basic, sensual way down below way.)

Social life active – but blahs – one nice thing – Marty (the professor you met) invited me to his sons Bar Mitzvah – Sam (Mr. Clean) too. Sweet! Ellen (my nun) is having a Halloween Party, so I will meet all her new way out friends. Sandy looks like a woman, a beautiful one. Believe it or not! A fall – wig – red dress – red cape – red lipstick – a real doll. Still working for C.P... Did you know that Norman Thomas graduated from Union Theological Seminary? Great people come from there. Laurie in Montreal.

Love,
L.

Thursday 8:30PM
Darling –

Sat down to catch up on my chores! Read thru my bills and decided not to worry about them tonight – the more pressing thing is my "Singles on the Left" involvement. I am the new chairman and must say that I find it a big responsibility. We want to continue the group but give it a new image, make it purposeful, etc. This on top of my work, yoga and social life is tough but I feel a responsibility to that segment of society (the older left singles in NY who have found it difficult to express themselves because most movements are in the hands of the youth). I will let you know if the project is fruitful! Personally I have met wonderful people and my life is the richer for it….

I drove out to Waldemar today to get advice from Florence on my work. She is a simply fantastic organizer… I'm growing to love my "ex nun" Ellen more and more. She has been exposed to a whole new group of international action people and is developing into a real radical. It's fun watching her awakening… Must sign off because of pressure of work. (Today I missed your comradeship as I shopped in the A&P.) How many ways I miss you.

Dear Tami –

Just a little note at the end of the day. Let us call it a Cancer Care Day in the life of Lucille Gold.

Arrived at work after forgoing a chance to do yoga at daybreak. I was just too muscle bound from last night's session at the Y. Breakfast at the Squire and up to my new office. Lunch in the 444 coffee shop. The purchase of a new powder puff and stamps and 10 post cards. Phone calls in and out about contracts for the Bklyn Benefit in May… How utterly horrible… The only relief was a phone call from Dr. Heigenson, my breast Dr. who called to apologize <u>personally</u> for having me pay twice. With all his work! And last, the viewing of our new film on our services. It is just marvelous. Color – beautiful music – the actual scenes of a family facing the horror of cancer in the home and how, with our help, the family is able to function. Wish the administration would make it more enjoyable for me because <u>we</u> <u>do</u> <u>serve</u>.

Love Mother

Thurs Nov 6, 1968
11PM
Dearest Tami –

It always seems like a long time between letters – that's because so much happens to me. I'll start with my this and that first!

Sal's girl Lisa – I met her Sunday. She is a good solid girl, I wish I could take her under my wing but alas, the timing is wrong. I'm not home enough.

Rhoda – I had a wonderful reunion with her Tues. We attempted to see the frescos at the museum but it was much too crowded. I went home with her and we just were like two little girls rediscovering each other. We walked in the woods with Che, her new dog, ate supper and then all our friends came to call. What a pleasant evening. I slept over and went to work from there. I'm home tonight (in N.J.) for the first time in 4 days.

Work. I am so busy with the paper, a membership drive, etc. that I don't mind it as much. But I am focused on next year's school. I think I would be broken if anything goes wrong. And I am concerned about the money. I called Gary Rosenberg a few times and he hasn't returned my calls. I must write to him because I imagine the arrangements must be made now. I'll let you know just as soon as I hear.

Yoga – I work out at least twice a week by myself. I sure enjoy my Wed. sessions at the Y. This week I stayed on without the others and went for a swim – then I walked to the N.Y. apt. and didn't I feel good. My weight is now 151 – starting to diet again after a rest of 2 weeks to allow myself to build up after the flu.

<u>Dad</u> – I called him and read your letter – he was sure pleased. But the letter is worn out, I read it to everyone I can corner. It sure is a different life without you. Now it's Laurie's turn to give me a hard time. She's up and down emotionally, calling me all day long. But she has a gay way of being a wreck and I'm able to take it.

<u>Jane</u> – wedding Feb 14th as you know but they have decided not to have a reception. I'm not sorry for that! When she gets back from her honeymoon I'll have a little party.

<u>The elections</u> – I'm too tired to go into details but

I didn't vote

First there was utter horror – now a wait and see attitude.

I'll get into this next time – but you'll have to wait! The weekend will be hectic – 4 shows, the frescos and maybe the Cloisters.

Tami I got the pictures of you taken at World Fellowship. Just great – I love you.

Take pictures

Lucille

Dearest – your inspired picture diary arrived and delighted me. How beautiful everyone and everything appears. I can't wait to see it and who knows – it just may be possible for me to come down. What with you finding me a barn to sleep in and Paul getting a free plane trip – all I will have to provide is a willing body... Ron – Ron – Ron... he is a devil, not calling me and not writing... but don't let it stop you from writing to him. Can't you just accept the fact that he can only function this way... <u>And your hating men!</u> How could it be otherwise – coming from my family. But please let us not be fatalistic. We have to fight what we know is wrong. Sure people are bad – both men and women, but they are also good! Society – Society – Bad society makes people suspicious, self-interested, deceptive. While we reject this evil and reject people who let society destroy them – don't let us become destroyed by wickedness. Love, understand and keep fighting against that bad little witch in you. When things go wrong in a relationship how easy it is to say, "It's because he's a man." Then you don't have to look at yourself – the other individual. Be patient – it will grow – the good will win out. <u>With struggle</u>.

Love
The woman

Monday 5:30 AM

Nov. 1968

Dearest Tami –

The garbage men have come and gone, leaving me awake and thinking of you... Another exciting weekend with so much to tell... But first let me respond to your beautiful letter about your adventure into Moralia... I know how frustrating it must be to read my letters, I will try harder to make them legible, but if it continues to be a problem let me know and I will type them. Naturally I prefer to write because I feel closer to you this way... You speak of your art teacher Alfredo Salze and I know how you must feel because on some occasions I have felt that way to people I admired. How unfortunate to waste the time you have with him for the separation is undoubtedly not understood by him and unwanted also. But alas, as you say, we cannot always solve things easily or quickly and must live with certain conditions for a while.

You question something I said about Ron and asked whether I used the word "forever" cynically. Tami, you know me not at all if you can ever wonder about me be cynical. I may question – I may see weakness – I may become disenchanted by someone but never cynical. To hate, to distrust, to be cynical is to be unthinking, without understanding and unloving. I love Ron and to some extent understand him... I spoke to his mother today. She says he has gained weight but has a lingering cold, which he neglects. I left a message to have him call me. Mrs. Clark sends her regards. We had a real mother-to-mother talk but I swore her to silence because I didn't want Ron to know and possibly be angry with me... The last thing in reference to your letter is your poem. You won't believe me I expect, but I used it Sat as a basis for my speech before 300 people at a Cancer Care luncheon. It is beautiful in total but I had to use only the 1st 2 lines – develop my ideas and then I concluded my remarks with your last lines "countless one." It was very moving. I believe I can make these speeches warm, emotional and demanding because I feel such deep conviction that people want to be good, that they understand me and are inspired to achieve higher goals. And of course, since I'm not ashamed of exposing myself, my emotions, I am able to reach out and communicate... It was a great letter Tami and I keep reading it, to myself and others.

Short Takes:

I bought new Pakistanian dresses and find myself wearing only them – I feel more true to my personality in something simple but <u>un-American</u>...

<u>Friday night</u>: Ellen Potter's (ex nun – now working with me) Halloween Party. Great – an ambassador from here, a consul from there, the head of a new experimental college at Fordham, black, white, yellow, young and ageless me! A marvelous assemblage and we danced madly to every beat in the modern mode. Age doesn't count, color or even political belief – only one thing dominated. Warmth and love. Oh how these people allow their sensual feelings out. I had a new beau there. He is Jamaican, nice, crazy about me and I'm still that cool cucumber... But Laurie's in love, or so she was yesterday. To a boy she met at a party Friday night. Laurie is having a ball! Meeting and really living – moving away from John...

Love,

Me

Wed 7:30 11-20-68

Your tired mother greets you between spurts of activity (a presidents meeting today and a speaking engagement in the BX tonight). I dragged out last year's thank you speech. How convenient – but what to do when I have to return to the chapter. —- Please inspire me again as you did when I went to the Linden Luncheon. Last night Sam and I had dinner at Mr. Richards and then we went shopping for you. How much fun it was buying the record – but the art store was closed. I returned today and bought the pen but the nibs were sold out so we called another store and they are holding 2 for me to pick up tomorrow... No comment on the record since I must first find a record player to try it out. What a life – no record player at our age of affluence... poor mother.

...I have an appointment to see about my scholarship... (<u>Next</u> <u>Monday</u> – Nov. 25 1:30 P.M.) Keep your fingers crossed. I'm living for that moment – when I go back to school.

Mother

Monday
Dec 30, 1968
Dear Tami –

<u>Rest at ease now</u>! I will try to make all the arrangement for Cuba at this end! Laurie will be with you on Jan 11. On her return the finishing details will be made. I will arrive about the 17th of February.

Glad you called Friday night even though the cost will be high. Please call when you need the support of home – no amount of money is excessive at such times. I am proud of your ability to have made it as well as you have. Remembering how far you have come in the last year makes me doubly proud. It is very hard to be away from home I know. I used to save my money for trips home from Elmira and Syracuse and I didn't have as much at home as you do.

Ron! I haven't spoken to him at all so don't think I influence him in any way. And as you said – how could I tell him to say he loves you! You just can't believe he loves you! Well – obviously he does! In his own special way – and isn't that nice that we each have our own way of loving! I hope some day you find someone who loves you in the way <u>you</u> want to be loved. Maybe it will be Ron – you can't tell.

Me? I am very happy – no special love but such nice friends – Sam – Sal – Ted – Burt and many new ones. Yesterday Marty (the Professor) visited with Helen – Sam and I made the rest of the party and it was a delight. We laughed from early morning until night. Marty and Sam are fun people. Sam is too immature for me – Marty too old, so I will keep looking… Our Christmas dinner was so happy with Grandpa and Sylvia and Barbara and Don and of course Edith, Hy, Jane and Paul and Laurie. Duck and all else great! If I could see you for a few hrs I would say my life was in every way great! No, 2 days! No, a week. But it won't be long and I'll be in your arms. Whenever I get very lonely for you I close my eyes and feel our last embrace as I said good-bye to you next to the car at Friends World College that Sunday night.

I love you my big one! Laurie said you gained weight! Please be careful. And watch your stomach. Remember – you are my whole life – I would die without you.

Love
M.

Dear Tami,

My frustration is growing because I don't hear from you. Surprisingly enough though, I'm not upset! I called Margarita today and she suggested that I send this letter to her to forward to you. I am not confident that my letters are reaching you.

I keep thinking that it will be only a short time till I have you in my arms again. Today Phoebe asked me to set my vacation schedule – I said it depends on you and they can fire me if they don't like it! So there!

Nothing much new! I haven't heard anything about my scholarship! Laurie is really emotionally upset but feels that now she will really work with her therapist! She and I have had a beautiful year together but now she feels that she must break away from me! So here goes! I know it is true but very hard for a mother to accept! Especially a mother who is alone. I don't see Jane at all – she is happy with Paul, living in her own sweet world. I don't mind our separation as I would if that would happen to you or Laurie. Still I had thought her marriage to Paul would bring us closer. Guess she can never forgive me. How sad for me.

Grandpa and Sylvia just got back from Florida looking good – Arthur and Nell coming to NY next week (Arthur just had a hernia operation). I don't see the rest of the family so there is no report! Daddy and Thelma doing just fine – new rugs in their Flushing apt. Gail is going to have a baby – they are moving back to NY. Haven't heard from Ron since Jane's wedding! I'm going up to Fellowship this weekend to plant and kiss the stove. Nina isn't getting married – don't know what happened! Steve Monconi is going into the service. (I'm on Weight Watchers – lost 8 lbs.) I'm missing you mucho! Margarita sends love – everyone sends love.

– Me

March 3, 1969

Dearest Tami –

At long last – my first letter from you. I guess you have begun to receive mine. Paul Cowan had already called me last week so I know that you were well and many other things. He was so enthusiastic and went on and on. How I loved it! His article appeared in the Village Voice (so very good). I bought many copies and gave them to everyone.

Quick takes –

I am well – resting much – reading! Soul on Ice (great), Vincent Van Gogh's letters to his brother. A truly beautiful friendship that lasted till death, both within months of one another. Vincent was turbulent – constantly searching – oh so torn always. Identified with the underdog.

Did you know they have a TV hero now "Under-Dog" – so funny to me.

…I'm taking Paul Cowan and his wife out to dinner next wk.

More – more – tomorrow because I'm beat.

Love Me

12:15 AM

Wed – Mar 5

Dear Tami –

Since I can't sleep – reading impossible – thinking only depressing – Oh! talk to Tami – that's the answer.

The sky was light blue tonight as I exited from my prison at 1 Park Av. How very nice – but then there is the drive to clear out of the city. It won't be long and I will be away from the soot and foul odors. Naturally I am anxious about a scholarship – but no matter, I'll leave NY one way or another. Naturally, much depends on you. I await your return and ask the question – what will you do next? Africa – college in the U.S. – home with me – work in New York. Whatever – I sure hope we will have time together for a while. Never thought of it until this very moment – what about planning to spend the first week of Sept with me somewhere – anywhere – World Fellowship in New Hampshire where it is wild and daring with its mountains and water, beautiful landscapes and marvelous antiquing — or easy living in – lets see – a beautiful out of the way cottage on the sea – surfing, swimming, snorkeling, eating, or… camping in the

Smokies or… well anyway – let's spend a week. …I'm so glad there won't be snow or skiing because there I simply draw the line.

With these nice thoughts my eyes begin to close and I happily put down my pencil – kiss you goodnight and look forward to the future.

Loving you mucho,
the Woman

Mar 5, 1969

Dear Tami –

I hope Señora Carolina does not become bored with my letters that she must transmit. But if she knew how happy my talking to you makes me she would relish her role… My good friend Ellen is back from her vacation in Puerto Rico and I'm again at peace. She fills a very important need in my life as I in hers. We gab on and on like two little hens, and I'm afraid with as much clucking and nonsense. She is part baby and part woman. I delight in her struggle to attain womanhood. It's a fun thing because she isn't emotionally sick – only retarded by a 10 year sidetrack with the church… Suddenly my anxiety for you has mushroomed… It is caused by two things: 1. Paul Cowan's attempt to ease me made me begin to worry about the very questions he raised. 2. Before I was so busy working to get you to Cuba – only now can I find time to worry. Housing I know you can deal with (after the barn). But food? Most important is people. Who, where, oh, my little baby – how varied your life has been and so young. But maybe it is with you as with me – I can withstand so very much because I have taken Grace's strength as my own, Sophie's love into my heart and to walk into the future I have but to remember that you will be in it and all is as it should be.

There is much to be said for a routine life. I have heard of people who spend 40 – 50 – 60 years doing the same thing day by day. How? The nearest I've known to a routine in my present life is eating breakfast at the Squire, roll – egg – coffee and then (refilled cup and cigarette) to the bantering exchanges of delightful Helen – our philosophical, cheerful waitress. That's the only pleasant thing I can count on in the course of the day. Then there is the telephone conversation with Laurie, she may be depressed half the time but she has such a cheerful way of being depressed. Must say she has been perfectly wonderful to me since you left – filling the terrible void. How wonderful that she could do it, not being resentful of my great, special attachment for you. You would truly love some of our Yoga nights. When you come home we'll let you join in, but (I say boastfully) you're going to be jealous when you see me tie myself up in knots. (Not to mention standing on my head) Ha! Ha!

I wish I could have children now that I am mature. What a difference. By the way – I think I have really grown mucho! Come home and try me out. I'll mind your kids. Have half a dozen.

Grandma,

the Woman

Sat. Aug 2, 1969
8 A.M. enjoying the
last of my days of
vacation (see last page)

Dear Tami –

Lying here in bed I think of our many struggles together – struggles for understanding! How frustrating – how much of a challenge – yet how worthwhile. One such struggle was on Norman and his feeling for Martin Luther King. Can you imagine the implication of your attack on his idol – the figure that he is using as a model – his alter ego. He must reject you if he is to keep his goal steady. All I suggest is that in everything we undertake we start on the realistic foundation. A bricklayer must work from a solid concrete base, a knitter must pick up the existing stitches. Dealing with human material we must always remember that defenses are the personality protectors – if we are to change attitudes and beliefs we must first reassure that we are not dangerous to the individual psyche. What good is it to spout phrases to closed off egos.

You may wonder about the slowness of this process for revolutionary change. Fortunately there are other forces at play. <u>Group</u> <u>Pressure</u>. A person, let us take Norman, will feel the effects of the broad student movement, the Panthers, etc. He personally experienced the success of a struggle for Black History in his school. All these things help to shore up his positive thinking and also make him available to new ideas and change. (By the way Marx identified this type of interaction in the social scene as leading to <u>qualitative</u> change in the revolutionary struggle.) But you will get to that when you study Dialectics.

Now to another thought! I must thank you – for one thing, your consideration on my last day with you – lunch – hated eating that big fat sandwich but loved sitting across the table from you – not distracted by many other people and things. But I thank you for something more. Your participation in the active concerns of our society keeps open the door of life for me. I shall always try to be equal to your friendship.

Love,

L